Contents

Contents cont ...

Preface

Successful English 3 Second Edition will help students in the third year of secondary school to improve all aspects of their English studies, providing an ideal preparation for the literacy component of NAPLAN. The book has been designed with flexibility in mind, and is divided into four sections: Grammar, Spelling, Comprehension and Writing.

Each section of *Successful English 3 Second Edition* can be worked through sequentially, used in conjunction with other sections, or individual units can be selected to support a particular class or student. The units are ideal for homework exercises or classroom use. Thanks to the new design, most activities may now be completed on the page, allowing more space for students' answers. Writing to be completed off the page is indicated by the [icon] icon.

Grammar

This section is designed to help students improve their grammar and writing skills. Each full-page unit begins with a brief and clear explanation of the point of grammar followed by a range of activities. All the basics of grammar are covered, and activities are fun and relevant, allowing students to practise grammar skills in context.

Spelling

This section will help students improve their spelling as well as build their vocabulary. Each full-page unit begins with a panel of words followed by a range of activities that require students to use words in context. Unit topics are engaging and aim to stimulate students' awareness in language and to develop a recognition of its dynamic nature.

Comprehension

This section is designed to help students improve their reading and comprehension skills. Each double-page unit presents a text followed by a range of questions. A wide range of text types is presented, including fiction extracts, news and magazine articles, instructions, letters, poems and advertisements. Passages are interesting and engaging, and can be used as the basis for further class activities.

Writing

This section will help students develop their writing skills. Each double-page unit examines a different technique or genre of writing and presents examples followed by a range of questions. A wide range of fiction and non-fiction text types are covered, including informative, narrative, descriptive, instructive and persuasive texts. The exercises include creative activities and real-life tasks that require students to develop specific writing skills.

Online Teacher Resources

Successful English 3 Second Edition also offers a range of online support material for teachers, available at **oup.com.au/SucEng3**. Here, teachers can easily access answers without the need of referring to a separate book, and download additional assessment resources ideal for preparation in the Language Conventions component of NAPLAN.

Acknowledgements

The author and the publisher wish to thank the following copyright holders for the reproduction of their material.

ACP Magazines for extract "Guy Sebastian: Like it like that', by Wendy Squires, from the *Australian Women's Weekly*, November 2009 issue; Rachel Carbonell for 'Global warming is a slow drip, drip, drip apocalypse', from *The Age*, 6 January 2009; Don Congdon Associates, Inc. for the extract 'There will come soft rains' by Ray Bradbury from *The Martian Chronicles*, © 1950, Doubleday; Jason Dowling and *The Age* for 'Three dead in first seven hours of the year' from *The Age*, 2 January 2009; Fremantle Arts Centre Press for extract from *Hidden* by Ron Bunney, 2000; The Herald and Weekly Times for the articles 'Dog days a delight' by Jacqui Hammerton, from *Herald Sun*, 28 December 2008, 'Hop into Hanoi' by Alan Hill, from *Herald Sun*, 7 September 2001, 'School of hard frocks' by Susie O'Brien, from *Herald Sun* 13 January 2009, 'Stone Age Bodies' by Fay Burstin, from *Herald Sun*, 17 July 2005, 'Survival of the meanest' by Greg Thom, from *Herald Sun*, 7 January 2009, Penguin Books UK for extract from *Flour Babies* by Anne Fine; Penguin Group (Australia) for extract from *Lockie Leonard, Human Torpedo* by Tim Winton, reproduced with permission; Royal Automobile Club of Victoria (RACV) Limited for 'RACV ballot', reproduced by permission; The Society of Authors as the Literary Representative of Estate of John Masefield for 'A Ballad of John Silver'.

Every effort has been made to trace the original source of copyright material contained in this book. The publisher would be pleased to hear from copyright holders to rectify any errors or omissions.

Heather McIntosh

Part 1
Grammar

This section introduces students to the essential rules of grammar, punctuation and word usage. Topics are introduced with a concise definition and clear examples, followed by a range of fun and engaging activities that allow students to consolidate their grammar skills and practise them in context. Each of the 34 grammar units is a stand-alone worksheet, so students can work through them sequentially or use them according to their needs.

Within each unit there is a range of activity types catering to a variety of learning styles. The exercises are graded within each unit and so will satisfy students of different levels. Sufficient writing space is included to ensure most activities may be completed on the page, but there are also extended writing activities to enable students to practise acquired skills in context. New revision units ensure students can confidently consolidate then extend their knowledge and skills. Exercises to be completed off the page are marked with the icon.

Grammar
Unit 1
Parts of speech revision 1

This unit revises **nouns** and **pronouns**.
- **Common nouns** name people, creatures, places and things, so they are the largest group of nouns.
- **Proper nouns** name specific people, places or things and always start with a capital letter. Note, however, that seasons and compass directions are not proper nouns.
- **Collective nouns** name groups of people, animals and things.
- **Concrete nouns** name physical, observable, touchable objects, animals and people.
- **Abstract nouns** name non-physical feelings, qualities, ideas, actions and states.
- You should be aware that some nouns may also function as a **different part of speech**:

Send me a *text*. (noun)	I'll *text* you. (verb)
Mrs Maynard is on maternity *leave*. (noun)	Don't *leave* your stuff there! (verb)

- Using a **very specific noun** is always better than using adjectives, general nouns or complicated explanations:

'Harry is a pessimist' is better than 'Harry has a tendency to expect and think the worst'

- **Pronouns** replace nouns to avoid repetition.

1 Highlight the abstract nouns in this word list and underline the concrete nouns:

admiration	affection	anger	annoy	annoyance	prosecute	Cinderella
confidence	cowardly	dependence	derringer	disinterest	Frankenstein	guava
justify	landing pad	prosecutor	love	lovely	Newcastle	ocean

2 Improve these sentences by replacing the italicised words with one of these nouns:

cathedrals	logbook	odometer	patricide	penultimate

a While in Europe we saw many *beautiful, great, big, old churches*. _____

b The defendant was found guilty of *killing his father*. _____

c Susie was sorry it was the *second last* day of school holidays. _____

d Before filling his car with petrol, my father always checks the *instrument on the dashboard that indicates how many kilometres he has driven,* and records the information in a *little book for that purpose*. _____ _____

3 Draw coloured lines matching each collective noun with the group it describes:

a	A scourge of	beauties
b	A prickle of	ducks
c	A crash of	tigers
d	A bevy of	hoodlums
e	A paddling of	unicorns
f	An ambush of	hedgehogs
g	A gang of	mosquitoes
h	A blessing of	rhinoceros

4 Highlight the nouns in this word list that should begin with a capital letter:

arabic	autumn	dollar	east	grandmother	greek	hydrogen
july	mars	milky way	napoleon	sony	south australia	star wars

Grammar
Unit 2
Relative pronouns

The **relative pronouns** *who*, *whom*, *whose*, *that* and *which* are **link words**. They link nouns with further information, which is provided by **clauses**. (A clause is a group of words within a sentence.)

- **Who** and **whom** refer to people.
  - *Who* is used when the noun is the *subject* of the sentence (the subject governs the verb):

The boy who won the race collapsed at the finish line.   (*The boy* is the subject.)

  - *Whom* is used when the noun is the *object* of the sentence (the object is governed by the verb):

I had a disagreement with a girl whom I dislike.   (*I* is the subject; *the girl* is the object.)

- **Whose** is used to show ownership or possession. Do not confuse it with *who's*, which is an abbreviation of *who is*:

We donated money to the people whose homes were lost in the bushfires.

- **That** and **which** refer to things.
  - *That* should be used when the clause helps to clearly define the noun:

The car that I wanted to buy had already been sold.   Ella chose the shoes that had the highest heels.

  - *Which* is used when the clause is not actually defining the noun but simply providing extra detail:

Beckham finally scored a goal, which relieved the team.   I downloaded Photoshop, which was recommended.

1   **Place the correct relative pronoun in the following sentences:**

   a   It was Atish _____ irritated Mr Geisler the most.

   b   It was George's pathetic attitude _____ irritated me the most.

   c   I did not tidy my room as requested, _____ displeased my mother.

   d   The clothes _____ my brother bought had to be returned.

   e   Tanya, to _____ I gave nothing, gave me a very generous Christmas present.

   f   It was Meera, _____ voice was the loudest, _____ grabbed our attention.

2   **Each of these sentences has words missing. They may be verbs, nouns or relative pronouns. Think of an appropriate word that fits the context:**

   a   _____, _____ is late all the time, actually arrived early for a change!

   b   I lost my _____ while I was skating, _____ was a real pity as I loved it.

   c   The dress _____ Stefanie chose had sequins all down the back.

   d   The dress I _____ to the wedding was identical to the bridesmaid's, _____
       was pretty embarrassing.

   e   The boy to _____ I lent my Geography notes quickly returned them, _____
       was a relief as I needed them for my homework.

3   **Only one of these sentences is grammatically correct. Tick the one you think it is:**

   a   Dennis, whose tall and built like a tank, can be quite intimidating when he's angry.   ☐

   b   The thing which I like to do on the weekend most, is go mountain bike riding.   ☐

   c   It was ironic that Hiro, whose party it was, fell asleep early and missed all the action.   ☐

Grammar
Unit 3
Interrogative pronouns

The **interrogative pronouns** 疑问(所疑问问问代词) *who*, *whom*, *whose*, *which* and *what* introduce questions. (To *interrogate* means to ask questions.)

- The pronoun **who** is used to refer to the subject 主语 in a sentence:

Who is sitting in my chair?

- The pronoun **whom** 他们 refers to the object 宾格 in a sentence:

Whom did you see?

- In modern, informal language, especially conversation, it is sometimes acceptable to use *who* instead of *whom*. However it is important that you know when to use *whom* correctly.
- **Whose** implies possession (do not confuse it with the contraction *who's*):

Whose keys are these?

- **Which** implies there is an obvious choice and *what* is used when there is no choice involved:

Which brand is more expensive?   What motivates you?

1 Complete the following sentences with an interrogative pronoun:

a _____ Who _____ won the raffle?

b _____ Which _____ colour are your eyes?

c _____ Which _____ dress do you prefer?

d _____ Whose ~~Whom~~ _____ car is blocking our driveway?

e _____ Whom _____ did you kiss?

f _____ What _____ are you doing?

g To _____ whom _____ are you speaking?

h _____ Which _____ way is it to the bank?

i _____ Whose ~~Whom~~ _____ bike is this?

j _____ Who _____ wrote this?

2 Highlight the correct word in the following sentences:

a (Whose, (Who's)) responsible for collecting the money?

b It was Jade's father (who, whom) volunteered to pick us up.

c To (who, whom) shall I give the cheque?

d You must return the wallet to (who, whom) it belongs.

e (Whose, Who's) picture do you think is the best?

f (Whose, Who's) going to have pizza?

g Ernest Hemingway wrote *For (Whom, Who) the Bell Tolls* in 1940.

h (What, Which) one is yours?

i To (who/whom) shall I bequeath my house?

3 Imagine that you are a police officer and that you have been sent to investigate one of the following crimes. Pick a crime and write twenty questions to ask the witnesses. All questions must begin with an interrogative pronoun:

- the theft of a Picasso painting from a gallery
- the kidnapping of a prize-winning poodle
- an altercation at a garage sale, resulting in two assaults
- the disappearance of a resident from a nursing home

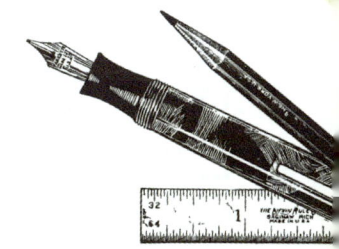

Grammar
Unit 4
Reflexive pronouns

> The **reflexive pronouns** *myself, yourself, himself, herself, itself, ourselves, yourselves* and *themselves* refer back to the subject in a sentence. (Remember, the subject is the noun that governs the verb.)
>
> I hurt myself.   Please make yourselves at home.   They only have themselves to blame.
>
> Reflexive pronouns cannot be used as the actual subject in a sentence:
>
> Incorrect: Neerja and myself attended the sale.   Correct: Neerja and I attended the sale.
> Incorrect: Rob fell in love with myself.   Correct: Rob fell in love with me.

1 Place the correct reflexive pronoun in these sentences:

   a I bought _____ a new Mac.

   b Roderick has really got _____ into serious trouble.

   c A chameleon can change its colour to disguise and protect _____ .

   d 'Boys, get _____ dinner please. I'm going out,' called Dad.

   e We dressed _____ warmly to brave the cold.

2 Highlight the correct word:

   a (You, Yourself) and Meg are my best friends.

   b The rules do not apply to (myself, me).

   c The chef bumped (his, himself) head on an open cupboard.

   d The chef hurt (him, himself) while preparing desserts.

   e Bella and Stella did not know what they were getting (herself, herselves, themselves, them) into.

3 Complete this paragraph by inserting appropriate pronouns:

I never wake up when _____ alarm goes off. _____ set it with the best of intentions, but I

can't wake _____ up enough to actually get out of bed. When _____ brother has heard

_____ alarm go off twice, he comes in and pulls _____ doona off. Once my feet are on the

cold wooden floor, it's easier to motivate _____ to get ready. I have a shower, brush _____

teeth, get _____ dressed and then go downstairs. I would be quite happy to make breakfast _____ ,

but Dad likes to make a big deal of the occasion. He cooks eggs and bacon, but Mum likes to make the tea _____

because she says Dad makes rotten tea. After breakfast I pack my bag, make _____ bed and get

_____ out the door before anyone asks me to help _____ little sister get ready. It's difficult

enough organising _____ , let alone organising someone else as well.

4 Write a paragraph about someone else's morning routine. Pick one of the following people and include at least five reflexive pronouns:

   • your grandfather   • a dairy farmer   • the Queen

   • an early morning DJ   • a soldier   • an adventurer climbing Mount Everest

Grammar
Unit 5
Using pronouns revision

This unit gives you an opportunity to cement your understanding of **pronouns**.

1 Change these sentences:

a *to the third person:* I am very happy with my exam results. _____

b *to the first person:* You kicked the door with all your might. _____

c *to the second person:* He is a troublemaker. _____

d *to the second person:* I should check my email every day. _____

e *to the third person:* You look great with your hair like that. _____

2 Fill in the gaps with *me, myself* or *I*:

a After dinner is finished, _____ have to pack the dishwasher.

b My mother asked _____ to unpack the dishwasher.

c _____ have been known to sing to _____ while washing the dishes.

d If it's just _____ at home, _____ leave the dishes until the next day.

e My Dad and _____ often chat about important stuff while we do the dishes.

3 Place a relative pronoun in the spaces provided:

a I'm not going to be lenient when I find the person _____ stole my Nintendo DS.

b We missed seeing her by five minutes, _____ was a real pity.

c Princess Diana was a woman _____ many people admired.

d Tim, _____ job it was to type up the letters, turned out to be a dreadful speller.

e I soon realised the goals _____ I had set myself were unachievable.

4 Highlight the correct interrogative pronoun:

a (Which, What) way do you think is the fastest?

b (Whom, Who) will take responsibility for showing the new kid around?

c (What, Which) are your intentions?

d (Whom, Whose) jumper is this?

e To (whom, who) are you sending those flowers?

5 Place a tick next to the grammatically correct sentence in each of these pairs:

a Miss Lee is the teacher whose most admired. ☐   Miss Lee is the teacher who's most admired. ☐

b Which hand-held game do you prefer? ☐   What hand-held game do you prefer? ☐

c Dan and I went psycho. ☐   Dan and me went psycho. ☐

d I will take responsibility for me. ☐   I will take responsibility for myself. ☐

e Please return application forms to myself. ☐   Please return application forms to me. ☐

f Japesh and I got caught. ☐   Japesh and me got caught. ☐

Grammar
Unit 6
Parts of speech revision 2

This unit revises **verbs**, **adjectives** and **adverbs**.

- **Verbs** are action words and indicate the tense of a sentence.
- The person or thing that carries out the action is the *subject* (a noun), and may be singular or plural. The verb must *agree in number* with the subject.
- **Adjectives** make writing interesting by describing nouns. They provide information about qualities such as size, shape, colour, number, taste, attitude, direction, age, weight and sound.
- **Proper adjectives** need a capital letter:

| Indian culture, | Roman Catholic mass, | Shakespearean style |

- **Quantitative adjectives** indicate how much:

| some people, | many mistakes, | all schools, | little expectation, | much debate |

- **Comparative adjectives** compare people and things.

| ugly, | uglier, | ugliest, | refined, | more refined, | most refined |

- **Adverbs** answer the *how, when* and *where* questions about verbs and are usually formed by adding 'ly' to an adjective.
- Adverbs can also provide more information about adjectives or other adverbs.

1 Rewrite these sentences in a different tense. Ensure the verb is altered correctly:

   a Their spaceship lands heavily. (*to the past*) _____

   b You were stunned. (*to the future*) _____

   c I was furious. (*to the present*) _____

2 Rewrite these sentences by changing the number of the subject. Again, ensure the verb is altered correctly:

   a My best friends are invaluable. (*to the singular*) _____

   b One man was severely injured. (*to the plural*) _____

   c I was protesting on principle. (*to the plural*) _____

3 Insert the correct form of comparative adjective:

Positive	Comparative	Superlative
	more impressive	most impressive
angry		angriest
disappointed		
	better	best
much	more	
	lonelier	

4 Change these adjectives into adverbs:

   a easy _____   **d** memorable _____

   b rebellious _____   **e** fishy _____

   c incessant _____   **f** domestic _____

Grammar
Unit 7
Infinitives

Infinitives are the most basic form of a verb. They have no direct relationship to time, person or number. Most infinitives in English begin with the word *to*:

to see, to dance, to cry, to have, to be able, to be, to perform, to moan, to gibber, to disarm, to pout, to mollify

- You may hear people say that you should never **split an infinitive**. This means that you should not separate the word *to* from the rest of the infinitive. Today, it is acceptable to split the infinitive; however it is probably best to avoid it in formal writing:

Instead of: We wanted to quickly run.   You should write: We wanted to run quickly.

- Infinitives are **non-finite verbs**, that is, they cannot stand on their own. They need an auxiliary verb to make sense:

Without an auxiliary verb: I to dance.   With an auxiliary verb: I like to dance.
Without an auxiliary verb: Adib to learn the drums. With an auxiliary verb: Adib wanted to learn the drums.

1 Highlight the infinitives in these sentences:

   a I wanted to do the tango, but Sophie wanted to rumba.

   b Nina was nervous because she had to sing in front of a thousand people.

   c Naveen had to continuously fight an irrational fear that while he was dissecting the worm it would start to wriggle.

   d Quentin would have liked to attend the science fair.

2 Complete these sentences by inserting an infinitive:

   a Jude had always wanted _____ to India.

   b In order to get what she wanted, Kylie knew that she had _____ her mother for days on end.

   c Alessandro's goal for the season was _____ 180 centimetres in the finals.

   d Wilma found it virtually impossible _____ the internet.

   e It is always far too easy _____ money you just don't have.

3 The following infinitives require an auxiliary verb in order to make sense:

   a I _____ to do housework.

   b She _____ to see for herself.

   c They _____ to fly to Paris for their anniversary.

   d I was _____ to miss my curfew by a long shot, so I knew Dad was

      _____ to clobber me when I eventually got home.

4 Rewrite these sentences to see if you can avoid committing the 'crime' of splitting the infinitive!

   a The dentist hoped to painlessly remove the tooth. _____

      _____

   b Wade loves to brazenly pick his nose. _____

Grammar

Grammar
Unit 8
Finite and non-finite verbs

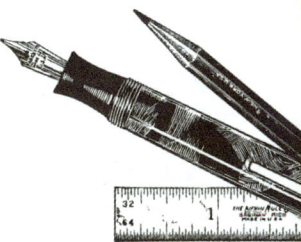

- Every sentence needs a **finite verb**, which is a verb that has a subject (a person or thing to carry out the action). A finite verb and a subject together will make sense—and indeed make a sentence—on their own:

| We sing. | She plays. | They travel. | The mouse nibbles. | I am. |

- A **non-finite verb** (also known as an **infinite verb**) does not make sense when used with a subject on its own:

| I to go | She to swim | I going | He sleeping | They having |

- Non-finite verbs need **auxiliary verbs** to help them make sense:
  - A non-finite verb plus an auxiliary is called a **verb phrase**.
  - A verb phrase and a subject create a sentence.

In the examples below, the auxiliary verb is in bold and the non-finite verb is italicised:

| He **wanted** *to go*. | She **hates** *to swim*. | They **are** *amazed*. | We **will be** *compensated*. |

- To test if a verb is finite, see if it can stand on its own with a subject:

He cooking.	(This does not make sense, therefore the verb is non-finite, and needs an auxiliary to make sense.)
He is cooking.	(This makes sense. There is a non-finite verb plus an auxiliary verb (verb phrase).)
He cooks.	(This makes sense, therefore the verb is finite. This is a sentence.)

---

1 Highlight the finite verbs in these sentences:

a Little Tommy Tucker sings for his supper.

b Should I go to school if I still have spots from the measles?

c I simply do not understand why you insist on shouting all the time.

2 Add a suitable auxiliary verb to the non-finite verb to create a verb phrase in the following sentences:

a He _____ to buy a new suit for the formal.

b Oscar _____ hoping to learn the piano, but his parents _____ insisting on the clarinet.

c Dean _____ planning to ask Daphne to marry him.

3 Add a suitable non-finite verb to the auxiliary verb to create a verb phrase in the following sentences:

a As a keen gardener, Mortimer likes _____ his garden to the public every spring. He loves

_____ the looks on people's faces when they see the tulips.

b I think he wants _____ with you!

c Basima is _____ her speech.

4 Highlight the correct form of the verb to complete these sentences:

a Human hearts (is, are) shaped like a pear.

b They (exercised, exercising).

c You (makes, make) me angry.

d The Moon (spin, spins, span) round on its axis in 27.3 days—exactly the same length of time that it

(take, took, takes) to (orbit, orbits, orbited) once round the Earth.

e Hemi will (decided, decide).

f I (have, has) remembered.

g Rafe has (seen, saw, sees) the light.

Grammar
Unit 9
Subject/verb agreement

A verb must agree with its subject in number, person and tense. This means that a singular subject needs a singular verb and a plural subject needs a plural verb. It also means that the person and tense must be the same for the subject and the verb:

I am furious. (*first person, singular, present*)   We are furious. (*first person, plural, present*)

You will be furious. (*second person, singular, future*)   You will be furious. (*second person, plural, future*)

She was furious. (*third person, singular, past*)   They were furious. (*third person, plural, past*)

- Even when a verb is separated from the subject to which it refers, it must still agree:

My cousins, who live overseas, are flying in for Christmas.

- A collective noun is singular if it refers to a whole group, but plural if it refers to individuals in a group:

Our school is very run down.   About half of the school are going to be there.

- Singular subjects joined by the conjunction *and* usually require a plural verb:

You and I are going to be good friends.   Roger and Rupert have the same rituals.

- When the subject is qualified by words such as *each, every, one, either, neither, anyone, everyone, nothing* or *something*, the verb is singular:

One of the apples was eaten.

- When the subject is qualified by words such as *all, some, many, more, few, most, several* and *both*, the verb is plural:

All of the apples were eaten.

1 Complete the information in this table:

	Person	Number	Tense
I will be relieved when it's all over.	first	singular	
It was amazing they all survived.		plural	
He and Jane dance well.			
You are my heroes!			present
A lazy flock of sheep ambled past them.	third		
About a third of the flock escaped.	third		past

2 Complete these sentences by inserting suitable verbs:

a   We _____ going to hitchhike but thought it was probably too dangerous.

b   Each of the representatives _____ to make a speech yesterday.

c   Ewan discovered all of his crayons _____ missing.

d   My hockey team _____ completing a tour of Scotland in July.

3 Change these sentences …

a   *into the third person, plural*: I am eating my favourite meal. _____

b   *into the future tense*: We went shopping on Saturday. _____

c   *into the second person, singular*: Lara thinks she is a bad person, but she isn't. _____

d   *into the past tense*: You will be well behaved and polite. _____

e   *into the first person, plural*: I am nervous about my interview. _____

Grammar
Unit 10
Verbs and tense

You are aware of the three simple tenses: *past*, *present* and *future*. These can be further divided:

- **Perfect tenses** indicate an action is completed (or **perfect**). They are formed by using a form of *to have* plus the **past participle** of the verb:

Past perfect: I had walked.   Present perfect: I have walked.   Future perfect: I will have walked.

- **Continuous tenses** (also known as **progressive tenses**) indicate that an action continues. They are formed by using a form of *to be* and the **present participle** of the verb:

Past continuous: I was walking   Present continuous: I am walking   Future continuous: I will be walking

- It is crucial that the same tense is used throughout a piece of writing; however, within a given sentence, you may need to use different tenses:

We were sleeping when the alarm sounded.

1 Insert the correct form of the verb *to have* into these phrases to form the perfect tense:

a *past:* I _____ danced

b *present:* We _____ seen

c *future:* You _____ gained

d *past:* She _____ laughed

e *past:* It _____ occurred

f *future:* They _____ agitated

g *present:* I _____ umpired

h *future:* I _____ umpired

i *past:* We _____ crossed

j *future:* It _____ been

2 Insert the correct form of the verb *to be* into these phrases to form the continuous tense:

a *present:* I _____ meandering

b *future:* They _____ missing

c *past:* We _____ viewing

d *present:* I _____ mocking

e *future:* You _____ hosting

f *past:* He _____ turning

g *past:* She _____ regarding

h *past:* We _____ conducting

i *future:* It _____ raining

j *present:* It _____ producing

3 Identify the tense of the italicised words in these sentences:

a To prepare for the marathon, I *am running* every morning. _____

b They *had concocted* a ridiculous story to cover up their mistake. _____

c Throughout this trial, Elisabeth *has impressed* us all. _____

d It *will be depending* on what the boss says. _____

e He *was trying* so hard not to laugh, he was going red in the face. _____

f Liz *will be acting* on your behalf. _____

g We *are hoping* to finish the project by mid-May. _____

h You *were running* from your responsibilities, Giovanni. _____

i Next month, we *will have* a party to end all parties. _____

j I think this infection *has run* its course. _____

Grammar
Unit 11
Active and passive voice

- The **active voice** is where the subject in a sentence *carries out* the action:

  Blake *threw* the tennis ball. (*Blake* is the subject.)

- The **passive voice** is where the subject in a sentence *receives* the action:

  The tennis ball *was thrown by* Blake. (*The tennis ball* is the subject.)

- Passive verbs are either accompanied by the word *by* or the word *by* is implied:

  The scrumptious wedding cake was quickly consumed. (The words *by guests* are implied.)

- In general, it is more effective to use the active voice because it is more concise, easier to understand and more personal. However the passive voice is useful in report writing and formal, official texts when the writer wishes to sound objective:

  Passive: The station was spray-painted by vandals.   Active: Vandals spray-painted the station.

- Often the spelling and grammar checker in a word-processor informs you that you should use the active voice. This means it recommends that you reverse the subject and object in your sentence and remove the word *by*.

1   Complete this table (the first one has been done for you as an example):

Active voice	Passive voice
Lowanna brought the salads.	The salads were brought by Lowanna.
	Three goals were scored by Amanda.
A passing car ran over his dog.	
	Lunch was carried in by a cheerful nurse.
Sonya Freedman replaces the retiring mayor.	
	Our house was rid of ants by an exterminator.

2   Are the following sentences written in the active or passive voice?

   a   The ferocious winds damaged many homes. _____

   b   Broth is spoiled by too many cooks. _____

   c   The media exaggerated the man's injuries. _____

   d   Pasteurisation was invented by Louis Pasteur. _____

   e   Many asthma sufferers are affected by worsening pollution. _____

3   Rewrite the following sentences, changing them from passive to active.

   a   10 000 tonnes of crude oil was spilt into Bass Strait by a German tanker. _____

   _____

   b   An innovative and effective restructure was implemented by the new owner. _____

   _____

   c   Our shirts and skirts were neatly ironed by our industrious house-keeper. _____

   _____

Grammar
Unit 12
Using verbs revision

> This unit covers all aspects of using **verbs**.

1 Answer these questions:

a How must a verb agree with its subject? _____

_____

b What is the difference between perfect and continuous tenses? _____

_____

c What is a non-finite verb? _____

_____

d Why are auxiliary verbs sometimes called 'helping' verbs? _____

_____

e Most infinitives begin with which word? _____

2 Complete the following sentences by inserting one of the following verbs (one of them is used twice):
have, is, published, publishing, was, will, would.

a During the eighteenth century, English agriculture _____ revolutionised.

b Next year, Hanako _____ hoping to go overseas on a student-exchange program.

c Doctor Guy _____ be signing his recently _____ book.

d We understand you _____ prior experience. _____ that correct?

e Tanya _____ like to work in _____ when she finishes her degree.

3 Rewrite this text in the first person, past tense:

He creeps out of the change room, glancing around to see if anyone is looking at his swimming costume. No-one is. He scoots past the reception area and along the slippery, wet tiles towards the deepest end of the pool, where he flings himself in before someone from school spots him. He feels relief. He has made it. He slowly starts to swim. He takes long, deliberate, relaxed strokes and reaches the end in no time. He is a good swimmer and swims thirty laps easily. On the next lap, he starts to worry about facing that long journey back to the change room again.

4 Change these sentences …

a *to the active voice:* The hostages were held at gunpoint by the terrorists for three days. _____

_____

b *to the past continuous:* We rode our bikes hard and worked up a decent sweat. _____

_____

c *to the past perfect:* Ari was competing in the State team and doing well. _____

_____

Grammar
Unit 13
Parts of speech revision 3

This unit revises prepositions, conjunctions, interjections and articles.

- **Prepositions** connect nouns with other words. They usually precede the noun they govern and together they form a **prepositional phrase**.
- **Conjunctions** join words, phrases, clauses and sentences.
- Some conjunctions appear in pairs:

not only/but also	both/and	either/or	neither/nor

- Note some words may act as more than one part of speech. *Until*, for example, may be a preposition or conjunction.
- **Interjections** are informal words 'thrown' into sentences. They are often used to show emotion and sometimes sound like everyday speech:

oops, yuk, ow, ouch, wow, whew, ugh, hi, cheers, eh?, hurray, mm, sh! tut-tut, aha, alas

- **Articles** define nouns. The definite article *the* refers to a specific noun.
- The indefinite articles refer to any general noun:
  - *a* precedes consonant sounds
  - *an* precedes vowel sounds, including words beginning with a silent 'h'.

1 Create a prepositional phrase by adding either a noun or a preposition to the following:

a towards _____ **c** against _____ **e** _____ midnight

b _____ Tuesday **d** _____ the gym **f** under _____

2 Complete these sentences by inserting an appropriate conjunction:

a Neither snakes _____ spiders bother me.

b _____ you went into space unprotected, you would explode before you suffocated.

c _____ it's gross to visualise, it is true that a sneeze travels at 600 miles an hour.

d _____ you ask nicely, I'll lend you money, _____ don't ask me

again, _____ I can't afford any more.

3 Write three sentences containing two interjections each.

4 Complete these proverbs by inserting appropriate articles:

a _____ rolling stone gathers no moss.

b At _____ great bargain, pause.

c As cross as _____ bear with _____ sore head.

d _____ devil always leaves _____ stink behind him.

e _____ end justifies _____ means.

f _____ ill wound is cured, not _____ ill name.

g _____ iron hand in _____ velvet glove.

h _____ bird in _____ hand, is worth two in _____ bush.

i _____ Englishman's house is his castle.

j As nimble as _____ cow in _____ cage.

k Do not keep _____ dog and bark yourself.

l _____ fool and his money are soon parted.

m _____ more danger, _____ more honour.

n _____ old head on young shoulders.

o _____ bad workman quarrels with his tools.

Grammar
Unit 14
Coordinating conjunctions

- **Conjunctions** join words, phrases, clauses and sentences. They are used to link ideas and create variety in sentence length.
- **Coordinating conjunctions** join units of equal status; that is, where each part of the sentence is as important as the other:

> I go to the gym so that I can look like Arnold Schwarzenegger.   He's rich but generous.
> Would you prefer a BMX or a horse?

- Coordinating conjunctions include *and, nor, but, for, yet, or* and *so*. Note that *neither* usually accompanies *nor*, and *either* usually accompanies *or*.

1 Complete these sentences by inserting an appropriate coordinating conjunction:

a I can't decide whether I want to live in Adelaide _____ Perth.

b Denise _____ Hue-Lan moved over to make room for Cynthia.

c I rang _____ you obviously weren't home.

d She walked through the valley of death _____ she feared no evil.

2 Use a coordinating conjunction to join these sentences. You may need to alter the sentence slightly:

a Katrina is addicted to chocolate. She is also addicted to coffee. _____

_____

b Fergus can run fast. I can run faster. _____

_____

c Apparently it's going to snow next week. I might go skiing. _____

_____

d How can you be so nice to others? You are so rude to me. _____

_____

e Do you want to stay? Perhaps you want to go. _____

_____

3 Draw coloured lines matching a group of words from the left, a conjunction from the centre and a group of words from the right to form grammatically correct sentences:

a	It is important to prune roses	but	hear properly.
b	After the accident he couldn't see	and	I are interested in chess.
c	Her judgments were harsh	so	farcical scheme.
d	Her eyes were deep blue	yet	go for a bike ride.
e	Neither Timothy	or	you expect me to trust you.
f	You constantly tell lies	and	I'm not sure.
g	It's a ridiculous	or	they can quickly bloom again.
h	We've got time to either see a movie	but	fair.
i	I think Faruq wants to dump me	nor	seemed to look into my soul.

Grammar
Unit 15
Subordinating conjunctions

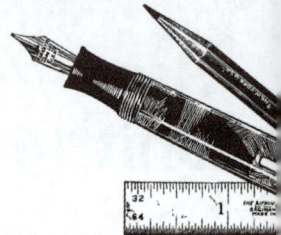

Grammar

Subordinating conjunctions introduce a subordinate clause; that is, a clause that is less important than the principal clause:

I'm happy to drive *as long as* you navigate.
Let's tidy the kitchen *before* Mum comes home.

In the above examples, the words in italics are the subordinating conjunctions and the words in bold are the principal clauses. The conjunctions introduce extra information about the principal clause.

Some subordinating conjunctions are:

after	although	as long as	as though	because	before	even
if	if only	in order that	once	rather than	since	so that
when	whenever	where	whereas	while		

---

1   Circle the subordinating conjunctions in these sentences, underline the principal clauses and highlight the subordinate clauses:

   a   I'm quiet and shy whereas my twin brother is loud, gregarious and bossy.

   b   Francis liked to write her essays quickly, rather than worry about spelling and grammar.

   c   Roy has become depressed and withdrawn since his wife passed away.

   d   After the storm, the SES had to clear the road of fallen trees and debris.

   e   I'd go swimming if only I didn't have all this work to do.

   f   Because of recent terrorist attacks, airport security has been tightened.

   g   Despite all hearsay, it is not particularly dangerous to swallow chewing gum, even though it is indigestible.

2   Insert one of the following subordinate conjunctions into each of these sentences: *although*, *as long as*, *if*, *so that*, *whenever*.

   a   I'll drive you to the party _____ Jakub's parents pick you up.

   b   I always get flustered _____ there are boys around.

   c   Reorder your paragraphs _____ the essay flows logically.

   d   What would you say _____ Brydie asked you out?

   e   _____ you put in more effort than last time, your grade is still too low.

3   Complete these sentences by adding an appropriate subordinate conjunction and an appropriate subordinate clause:

   a   We missed the beginning of the concert _____

   b   Ngai bullied everyone around _____

   c   They agreed to disagree _____

   d   Would you consider joining the army _____?

   e   _____ I will go crazy.

   f   _____ Candice was a hairdresser.

Grammar
Unit 16
Conjunctions and commas

Commas sometimes accompany **conjunctions** to make sure the meaning of the sentence is clear. When you use conjunctions, keep in mind these rules about commas:

• A comma precedes a coordinating conjunction unless the sentence is very short:

I'm going to be very late, but it just can't be helped.

• A comma is used after introductory words to ensure there is no ambiguity:

No matter how hard he punched, Jelani just couldn't knock his opponent down.

• A comma is used before conjunctions, such as *and* and *but*, when they are part of a long, complicated sentence:

Trudy and Jody decided to invite Kathy, Milly and Katy, but not Stacey, Cindy and Lindy, and definitely not Wendy or Shelly.

Do not forget that the purpose of a comma is to help make the meaning of a sentence clear, so if you feel one is necessary, then use it.

1   Make these sentences easier to understand by inserting commas.

   a Taro was grounded but he wasn't angry because he knew he deserved it.

   b After avoiding a tree and a telephone pole the car skidded to a violent halt.

   c Since the embargo was lifted relations between the two nations have improved.

   d While you sit around feeling sorry for yourself I'll see what can be done.

   e If all parties agree to our conditions the contract can be signed tomorrow.

   f Click on the link below to seek further information order or cancel items change your details reset your password and find our contact details.

   g As long as you live in my house you and your sister will abide my rules.

   h The ball was confidently kicked toward our goal but the keeper cleverly blocked it with a powerful header which is his famous and feared trademark.

2   Demonstrate your ability to identify conjunctions by highlighting all coordinating and subordinating conjunctions in the sentences in Exercise 1.

3   The following text is repetitious and long-winded. Rewrite it, inserting appropriate conjunctions and some commas to make it more readable. Some sentences may need to be altered significantly.

The following statement is the complete truth. I can't swear that I saw everything. I was slightly intoxicated. I left the restaurant. I had been celebrating my birthday. I walked along Simpson Road towards my house. I saw a black Holden ute travelling in a northerly direction. I noticed it was going very fast. I'd guess the ute was doing about 90 kilometres per hour. I'm not one hundred per cent sure. You can never really tell, can you? The ute passed me. I heard loud tooting. I heard shouting. I heard a horrendous smash. I ran over to see if I could help. The ute had hit a little red Mazda. The driver was okay. He was upset and shaking. Suddenly, two boys crawled out of the ute. They ran away. I didn't have time to grab them. One boy was tall. He was wearing a red top. The other one was skinny. He had long hair. It was dark. I couldn't see much. I can't give you more details. Sorry.

Grammar

This unit revises capital letters, full stops, exclamation marks, question marks, commas and ellipsis points.

- **Sentences** must begin with a *capital letter* and end in one of three ways:
  - with a *full stop*
  - with one *question mark* if a direct question has been asked, or
  - with one *exclamation mark* to indicate a command or strong emotion.
- Full stops are also used in *abbreviations* to show letters are missing (in this context, they are called *points*):

Sat. (Saturday)	a.m. (ante meridiem)	e.g. (exempli gratia, which is Latin for *for example*)
etc. (et cetera)	W.H.O. (World Health Organization)	

- A point is not necessary if the last letter of the abbreviation is the same as the last letter of the original word:

Mr (Mister),	St (Street),	Dr (Doctor),	Col (Colonel)

- **Commas** are used in various ways:
  - to separate items in a list
  - to separate elements of a sentence to avoid confusion
  - around words such as *therefore*, *however*, *finally* and *nevertheless* when they interrupt a complete thought
  - to mark a short, natural pause in a sentence where a reader may take a breath or pause
  - to separate the name of a person addressed, or described, from the rest of the sentence.
- Three points in a row are called **ellipsis points** and indicate whole words have been omitted:

'Is this a dagger which I see before me … Come, let me clutch thee.'

- Ellipsis points can also be used at the end of a sentence to leave it dramatically 'hanging in the air':

'But wait! There's more …'   'I am just going outside and may be some time …'

---

1 Rewrite these sentences so they are grammatically correct:

a   Do ~~do~~ you know what a palindrome is.
It

b   if you splash alcohol on a scorpion it will go mad and sting itself to death!!

c   I have seen war …. i have seen the dead in the mud.. I have seen cities destroyed ….. I have seen children starving I have seen the agony of mothers and wives I hate war (franklin d roosevelt)   *Franklin D Roosevelt*

d   *Let's* let's meet Meg Jai and Danny at 6 pm?

e   *Banning* ~~Banning~~ plastic bags from supermarkets would benefit marine animals such as seals whales and turtles many of whom die from ingesting plastic bags mistaken for food sources

---

2 Insert the necessary punctuation into these sentences:

a   If you are interested in applying for this position, please email a covering letter resume and three current references to our H R manager Ms Tabatha Fayne by 5pm on the 7th of Feb.

b   The most healthy productive soils are those that can hold water and release it to plant roots, Some soils like clay are full of water but it is trapped and plants cannot draw on it, In other soils such as sand the water flows quickly, through it not staying long enough to be of use to plants

Grammar
Unit 18
Punctuation practice 1

This unit tests your understanding of full stops, exclamation marks, question marks and commas.

1 Place a punctuation mark at the end of each of these sentences:

a   I wonder what Indah will say when I ask her to marry me, pondered Luke _____

b   'C'mon!' Henry shouted _____

c   In which stadium are the gymnastic events being held _____

d   I asked Julia to buy me cheap CDs, perfume and a watch while she was in Bangkok _____

e   The football coach demanded a significant pay rise, but the club committee thought that was pretty rich considering his team had not won a game in over five years _____

f   Should the legal drinking age be lowered to sixteen _____

g   'Scram _____'

h   I think I'll ask Mr Gill if I can have an extension on the History assignment _____

2 Place commas in their correct places in the following sentences:

a   The city lies quiet in a hot dusty brown twilight which smells of petrol frangipani and fear.

b   Dwarf planet Pluto has one large moon Charon and two small ones which are called Nix and Hydra.

c   I was struck by William's declaration. Like everything he said it was exaggerated but not blatantly false. He was boorish arrogant and dull but he wasn't a liar.

d   After the fireworks there were mounds of cardboard streamers burnt-out rockets used fuses and little red white and blue bits of paper lying all over the banks of the now quiet deserted river.

e   Moose the largest living deer live in the temperate forests of North America trampling the winter snow to find food.

f   Spacious and stylish this freestanding architect-designed four-bedroom three-bathroom residence boasts ocean views a three-car lock-up garage an outdoor spa and lap pool surrounded by manicured gardens and three enormous living areas.

3 Punctuate this text using full stops, commas and capital letters:

Simon walked slowly along the footpath looking into all the shop windows He wasn't sure what he was going to buy but he knew it was going to knock the socks off gabbie She always bought him really cool presents that made him feel pretty pathetic disorganised and thoughtless This time he vowed would be different It was her birthday next week and he was determined to impress her He had been saving for weeks doing jobs for his parents around the house and nagging uncle pete for money instead of the usual extravagant chocolate bars He had mowed the lawn cleared the gutters taken out the rubbish without being asked polished the silver washed both cars and even made dinner Once Simon would never admit it to anyone but he had actually enjoyed doing things around the house It was better than being bored anyway.

Grammar

This unit revises quotation marks, direct speech and paragraphs.

- **Quotation marks** are used to show someone is actually speaking (*direct speech*).
- All punctuation marks must be *within* the quotation marks:

'Out, damned spot!'

- Use **commas** to separate spoken words from unspoken words:

Hamlet declared, 'Frailty thy name is woman!'

- Start new sentences with a **capital letter**; but if a sentence is interrupted, use commas and no capital letter when the sentence resumes:

'But I will wear my heart upon my sleeve,' bemoaned Othello, 'for daws to peck at.'

- Always start on a **new line** when a new person starts to speak. This creates a new paragraph.
- **Indirect speech** does not require quotation marks because it is only a *report* of what someone said or thought.
- A **paragraph** is a group of sentences on the same topic, idea or point. Start a new paragraph by indenting slightly from the left-hand side of the page, or, if typing, by leaving an empty line.

1 Place a tick beside the grammatically correct sentence in the following pairs:

a The Minister for the Environment announced that, 'the desalination plant would go ahead despite protests.' ☐

The Minister for the Environment announced that the desalination plant would go ahead despite protests. ✓

b 'Truancy is a major problem,' said the Principal, 'But we plan to eradicate that within three years.' ☐

'Truancy is a major problem,' said the Principal, 'but we plan to eradicate that within three years.' ✓

c 'Why should a public building be sold for private profit?' asked a concerned resident. ✓

'Why should a public building be sold for private profit'? asked a concerned resident. ☐

2 Insert quotation marks into these sentences:

a Get up, stand up, sang Bob Marley. Stand up for your rights … don't give up the fight.

b Nichol agrees that keeping dogs inside has its pros and cons. 'Houses protect dogs from the elements, disease and potential fights,' she said, but it also means dogs do not get sufficient exercise.

c We need to accept that a pandemic in this country is a real possibility, read the Health Minister. However, there is no need for panic.

3 This text contains no paragraphs. Place an asterix where you think new paragraphs should begin:

'Thank you for attending this interview at short notice,' the manager started. 'You're welcome,' I said. 'I was very pleased to hear from you so quickly.' 'Could you tell us a bit about yourself?' she asked. 'Well, I have experience working in a busy office, because my Dad owns a small business, and he often lets me help out.' 'What's your Dad's name?' asked the assistant manager. 'Roger Doore,' I replied. 'Oh! I know your Dad well; he's one of our suppliers.' 'Yes, I know,' I said. 'That's how I know about this company and why I'd like to work here.' The manager glanced at her colleague, then smiled at me. 'That's nice to hear,' she said. 'When could you begin work?' asked the assistant. I tried to hide my excitement. 'School finishes in three weeks,' I said quickly, 'but I could work on the weekends if you need help earlier.' 'Excellent!' the manager quickly replied. 'That would be terrific,' the assistant joined in.

Grammar
Unit 20
Quotation marks

As well as indicating direct speech, **quotation marks** (which are sometimes called **inverted commas**) are used:

- to show someone or something is *being quoted*:

The Director of Public Prosecutions admitted the outcome was 'a travesty of justice'.

- to indicate the *names* of articles, chapters, poems, television and radio programs, songs, newspapers and magazines (just to confuse everyone, however, the names of major works—such as books, plays, operas, works of art and films—are in italics, not quotation marks; in handwriting, the italics are replaced by underlines):

My favourite poem would have to be 'The Road Not Taken'.

- with *foreign expressions*, *colloquialisms*, *made-up*, *special* or *unusual* words:

It seemed a 'fait accompli'.   He's 'done a runner'.   Do you know what 'hypnopaedia' is?   That's so 'povo'.

- to indicate a word, or its use, is *not the writer's own*:

Several 'experts' were called in. Yeah right …

These are formally referred to as **scare quotes** because they warn the reader that, in the opinion of the writer, there is something unusual, questionable or dubious about the quoted phrase. (Have you seen people in conversation raise their hands and twitch two curled fingers? That's a scare quote.)

---

1   Place quotation marks or underlining in their correct places in the following sentences:

a   The ambulance man said I was lucky to be alive.

b   Where would you find the statement An eye for an eye, and a tooth for a tooth?

c   We all started crying when they played Amazing Grace.

d   Who said, I bear a charmed life?

e   The manager said he would consider our application.

f   Your amazing idea, as you call it, has cost this company dearly.

g   Is it Reebok or Nike that uses the slogan Just Do It?

h   For homework, Leonie had to read I Love a Sunburnt Country.

i   Have you read Grisham's new book, The Law?

2   Place a tick in the box if you think the quotation marks in these sentences have been employed accurately:

a   I was so embarrassed when the DJ started playing 'Sweet Sixteen'. ✓

b   Do you know the proverb 'A lie begets a lie?' ⊗

c   Eliot wanted to finish 'The Lord of the Rings' before he saw the film. ✓

d   I usually find the articles in 'The Australian' quite interesting. ✓

e   Benjamin Franklin stated, 'There was never a good war or a bad peace'. ☐

f   The Minister for Foreign Affairs announced his visit to China was 'a success'. ☐

g   The highlight of our trip to Italy was seeing Michelangelo's 'David'. ☐

h   Dayaram was not happy about being dragged off to see 'The Pirates of Penzance'. ☐

i   We listen to 'The Bill and Ben Breakfast Show' every morning. ☐

Grammar
Unit 21
More about quotation marks

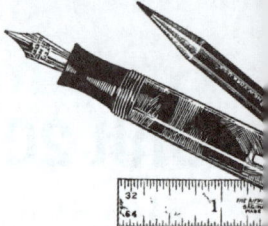

- The exact words of someone else, including relevant punctuation, are placed *inside* quotation marks.
- When quoting one line or less of text, the quote should simply be enclosed by quotation marks:

The poem 'Mental Cases' begins with the intriguing question 'Who are these? Why sit they here in twilight?' This first line immediately grabs the reader's attention.

- When quoting more than one line of text, however, the quote should be separated by starting a new line and indenting both sides of the page. Quotation marks are not used:

The poem continues to pose questions that become increasingly distressing. We begin to wonder who on earth these desperately unhappy and tortured souls are:

> Wherefore rock they, purgatorial shadows,
> Drooping tongues from jaws that slob their relish,
> Baring teeth that leer like skulls' teeth wicked?
> Stroke on stroke of pain,—but what slow panic,
> Gouged these chasms round their fretted sockets?

We soon discover the answers to these questions. These 'Mental Cases' are 'men whose minds the dead have ravished'.

- Three full stops are used to show words have been omitted from a quote. They are called *ellipsis points*:

The train continues on its journey 'towards the coppice where the withered oak leaves dropped noiselessly …'

1   **Place quotation marks in their correct places in the following sentences:**

a   The poem Morning Song opens with the happy statement Love set you going like a fat gold watch.

b   The Prime Minister revealed that he had no knowledge of that information …

c   The poet chooses to use unusual adjectives like clanks, thumped and chugs.

d   We are left with a powerful final statement: Rage, rage against the dying of the light.

e   The first line, Your nurse could only speak Italian, explains why words like Risorgimento and Dolce vita appear in this poem.

f   In Dawe's poem Homecoming, there is constant use of the word *they're*:

> *they're zipping them up in green plastic bags,*
> *they're tagging them now in Saigon, in the mortuary coolness*
> *they're giving them names, they're rolling them out of*
> *the deep-freeze lockers …*

Perhaps the speaker needs someone to blame for the sorrowful … mash.

g   Mrs Lawes, the NSW Police Commissioner, announced a crackdown on what she called an unacceptable and disturbing increase in drug trafficking.

h   In a letter to his friend, Abraham Lincoln wrote: I claim not to have controlled events, but confess plainly that events have controlled me …

i   I wonder how many people would agree that genius is one per cent inspiration and ninety-nine per cent perspiration?

Grammar
Unit 22
Punctuation practice 2

> This unit covers general punctuation but focuses on punctuating direct and indirect speech.

1 **Rewrite the following text, inserting paragraphs and quotation marks where necessary:**

I made a complete fool of myself last night. I tried to get into an R-rated film. I was so desperate to see Return of the Blood Sucking Bees that I threw all caution to the wind and went to the cinema armed with fake ID. May I have one ticket to Return of the Blood Sucking Bees please? I asked politely. Not on your life, buddy, came the quick-fire response. Pardon? I said. Not on your life, little man. Not unless you've got identification to say you're over eighteen. But I'm nineteen! I squeaked. Yeh, right sunshine. Where's the proof? I got out my recently acquired driver's licence with the cleverly altered birth date, and slid it under the thick glass. I was only shaking a tiny, weenie bit. The man didn't even try to cover his laughter. What happened to your sideburns? he guffawed. Sideburns? What sideburns? I thought desperately. Sideburns? Sideburns? Ah, those sideburns! The ones in the photograph I forgot to change. Oh, I don't believe it, I thought. How embarrassing. The man slid my plastic card back and said, Listen, mate, nice try. But you have to hop it, or buy a ticket to Bambi. Now what's it going to be? I turned and started walking away. Maybe I don't look much like my Dad after all.

2 **Each of the following sentences contains one grammatical error. Explain what is wrong with each one. The first one has been done for you as an example:**

a I asked my mum if she could pick me up early? → This sentence is a statement of fact, not a question that requires an answer. Therefore it should end in a full stop, not a question mark.

b Last night, I finally finished reading 'War and Peace'. _____

_____

c Francis said 'I'll love you forever, Frank!' _____

_____

d 'Help me!' cried the desperate man. 'I can't swim!!' _____

_____

e Don't forget to buy ham mustard and lettuce for my sandwiches. _____

_____

f 'Its amazing to see you again after such a long time!' exclaimed Winona. _____

_____

g 'I'm never going to clock this one,' thought Pramana. _____

_____

h We borrowed our friends caravan for the Christmas holidays. _____

_____

i In Act 5, Macbeth says, 'Life's but a walking shadow ... signifying nothing'. _____

_____

Grammar
Unit 23
Punctuation revision 3

This unit revises colons, semi-colons, brackets, dashes and hyphens.
- **Colons** introduce lists, quotations and definitions.
- **Colons** also join parts of a sentence. The information that follows a colon is usually an explanation, or elaboration of what precedes it.
- **Semi-colons** link statements that are closely associated or that complement or parallel each other in some way:

I will set up the Bunsen burner; you get the test tubes.

- Semi-colons can also separate long, complicated lists, which may already contain commas—the semi-colons mark a stronger division than that provided by commas, and avoid confusion. Note that a semi-colon is placed before the last *and*.

I feel pretty prepared for my exams: I have re-read my Geography, History and PE notes; I finished reading that ridiculous book for English, even though I hated it; I have asked Dad to help me with the Maths stuff I missed when we were on holidays; and I have borrowed Zac's Art History assignment, because he got an A, and I failed mine.

- **Brackets**, or **parentheses**, show that extra information or an afterthought has been added to a sentence; however the sentence is grammatically correct without it. No punctuation is necessary unless the brackets contain an entire sentence.
- **Dashes** emphasise additional information. They are often used in pairs like brackets. They can highlight a word or phrase at the end of a sentence by inserting a pause and creating a special effect.

I am so happy—not!

- **Hyphens** are smaller than a dash and join words, or parts of words, into compounds.

1 Label each of these statements *true* or *false*:

   a You should always ensure punctuation marks are inside brackets. _____

   b Using a dash at the end of a sentence is an effective way of creating a pause and highlighting information. _____

   c A semi-colon can create a stronger pause than a comma. _____

   d A semi-colon is half a colon. _____

   e A semi-colon can link two, closely associated statements. _____

   f Colons can be useful for introducing long lists. _____

   g If you place a dash between two words, you create a compound. _____

   h Brackets and a pair of dashes operate in a similar way by inserting additional information into a sentence. _____

   i Semi-colons introduce quotations. _____

2 Insert appropriate punctuation into these sentences:

   a A typical soil profile has a layer of humus decaying plant material at the top

   b We specialise in laser tattoo removal all colours anti wrinkle injections and non surgical facelifts

   c An interesting but useless fact it is impossible to lick your own elbow

   d My favourite foods are hamburgers from a fish and chip shop Tim Tams but not the dark chocolate ones my Grandma's butterfly cup cakes apple pie lamingtons and vanilla slice croissants from the French patisserie around the corner from my house sausages in white bread and pavlova but not when it's got banana on the top

Grammar
Unit 24
Punctuation practice 3

> This unit focuses on commas, semi-colons, colons, hyphens, brackets and dashes.

1 Make these sentences grammatically correct by inserting commas, semi-colons and colons in the appropriate places:

   a Only I know that my secret box contains the following an old two-dollar note some gold earrings I stole from my sister a photo of my dog Rex when he was just a puppy the ribbon I won for coming third in the school swimming sports in Grade 4 a snippet of my baby hair when it was first cut a *Mr Men* book I can't bear to throw out and a diary.

   b This is probably one of the most annoying proverbs I know 'Do as I say not as I do'.

   c Oliver must stay here you may go.

   d We had a dreadful trip down to the beach Dad played his old Buddy Holly tapes the whole way.

   e Elroy was pleased with himself he'd only received three detentions this week.

2 Rewrite the sentences in the left-hand column, inserting the appropriate phrase in brackets from the right-hand column:

   a Amira's grandmother was an amazing woman.   she's my best friend

   b Please hand in your rough drafts to me by Friday.   who passed away in 1996

   c Before starting to cook, make sure the eggs are at room temperature.   finished or unfinished

   d Andrea rings me every night and we chat until Mum shouts   Eggs will not whip up properly when cold.
       at me to get off the phone.

   a _____

   _____

   b _____

   _____

   c _____

   _____

   d _____

   _____

3 Insert hyphens and dashes into these sentences to make them grammatically correct:

   a Richard couldn't believe the figures written on the cheque ten million dollars!

   b Justin lacked self confidence.

   c Krishnan was always happy to help out the Star Foundation a non profit making organisation.

   d My mother in law a seasoned bargain hunter always spots the red hot specials.

   e The vice president of the footy club a non smoker was the one who suggested we ban smoking in the clubrooms.

Grammar
Unit 25
Using apostrophes revision

Grammar

> 1 **Apostrophes** are used to indicate ownership (the *possessive case*):
>
> Dion's nightmares,   the week's end,   some chefs' recipes,   sheep's pen,   the eggs' rotten odour
>
> • Remember to:
>   – add 's to singular words (an hour's time)
>   – add 's to plural words that do not end in 's' (men's business) and
>   – add an apostrophe when a plural word ends in 's' (ladies' night).
> • If a singular word ends in 's', and adding another one would sound clumsy, then you may leave off the extra 's'
>   (Jesus' feet).
>
> 2 Apostrophes are also used in abbreviated words to show that letters have been omitted (called **contractions**):
>
> 6 o'clock,   haven't,   isn't,   she's,   we've,   the door's busted,   the kid's gone crazy
>
> Remember:
> • Do not confuse the personal pronoun *its* with the contraction *it's*.
> • It is best to avoid contractions in formal writing.
> • Apostrophes are not used with numbers and dates (1980s, under 10s and 12s) unless it needs to be shown that
>   numbers have been omitted (everyone loves '80s music).

1 Place apostrophes in their correct place in the following phrases. (Be careful! Not all of them need an apostrophe.)

a the priests hassock

b a correspondents reports

c a countrys rights

d some countries rights

e vultures meal

f ladies purses

g a fellows got to be happy

h mens hairstylist

i Bob Jones truck

j the letters publication

k the accommodations appalling

l the antidotes strength

m the antidotes not working!

n all antidotes were tested

o a houses heating

p many houses floors

q the robot lifted its leg

r a soldiers story

s our Headmistress speech

t Shakespeares sonnets

u its a pity Jills parents cant stay

2 Place apostrophes in their correct places in the following sentences:

a 'The photocopiers broken again!' shouted Danijas secretary.

b The womans details were released by police today.

c The gamekeepers areas of responsibility include Lord Farquhars fields, ponds and woods.

d Dianas chihuahuas rheumatism became worse in the winter.

e 'You cant tell me shes innocent!' barked Bradleys Dad. 'Shes got 'guilty' written all over her face!'

f 'Theyre in the bottom drawer of Peters wardrobe,' said Mrs Orlowski, 'where theyre supposed to be.'

g Violets violets were violently violated.

h 'A blokes entitled to a moments peace isnt he?' demanded Bruce.

i The cooks efforts werent appreciated by the unruly mob of diners.

j Sauls swearing and sense of humour clashed with his girlfriends parents sense of decorum.

Grammar
Unit 26
Writing sentences 1

- A sentence must:
  - begin with a capital letter
  - end in a full stop, question mark or exclamation mark
  - contain at least one finite verb and a subject
  - consist of one main idea and
  - make sense in its own right.
- Sentences may be:
  - **simple** (consist of one main clause) or
  - **complex** (contain a main clause plus one or more subordinate clauses).
- **Conjunctions** are often used to link one clause to another.
- **Phrases** are used to add information and variety to a sentence. Unlike clauses, they do not contain a finite verb.

1   Name these groups of words. Are they simple sentences, complex sentences or phrases? Also, highlight all the conjunctions.

   a   Joey felt proud. _____

   b   Joey felt proud because he'd scored the winning goal. _____

   c   They played Scrabble all night. _____

   d   Playing Scrabble all night. _____

   e   Even though he felt tired, Santo took the dog for a walk. _____

2   Choose one of the following phrases to add to the sentences below: *by the lake, you bought last week, the new PE teacher, like a mad thing, reaching for the remote control.*

   a   _____, Yusef knocked over his hot chocolate.

   b   Miss Prince, _____, seems very strict.

   c   Will pedalled, _____, and launched his bike up and over the steep jump.

   d   That new lipstick _____ really suits you.

   e   The triathlon will start _____.

3   Rewrite these simple sentences to make complex ones by adding a subordinate clause, either at the beginning or end:

   a   Rollerblading can be fun.   d   I still love him.

   b   Plants need sunshine.   e   Georgia went for a quick run.

   c   Venice is a magnificent city.   f   We were late.

4   Turn the following groups of words into proper sentences by adding either a punctuation mark or a single word:

   a   Why didn't you tell me this before _____   d   _____ ate the meal silently.

   b   Quentin _____ a truck driver.   e   The Queen _____.

   c   Dharma gave it her best shot _____ it wasn't good enough.

Grammar
Unit 27
Writing sentences 2

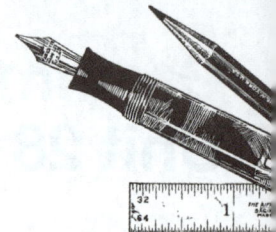

Sentences should only contain *one main idea*. Be aware, however, of having too many short sentences together, or writing a long, complicated, confusing sentence that would be better split into two or three separate sentences. Varying sentence length can help create atmosphere and make an impact on the reader.

To improve the overall quality of your sentences, review them carefully:

- Remove unnecessary words and avoid boring repetition.
- Check that your sentences 'sound right'. Sometimes altering the order of words can make a sentence more clear and effective.
- Remember that you can vary your sentence beginnings—you can start a sentence with an adjective, adverb, noun, participle, verb, phrase or clause.

1   These small paragraphs contain sentences that are either too long or too short. Rewrite them.

a   The bell for the second round went. The kid came at me fast. He hit me hard in the chest. It was not hard enough to knock me down. I saw a straight left coming from a mile off. I flicked my head slightly. It missed by a fraction. The crowd roared.

b   Every item of clothing you ever wanted to buy, but couldn't afford, is in the town of Milan, but be warned, you need to carry out some heavy-duty legwork before you are able to buy confidently, as there are more rip-off merchants willing to help you part with your money, than you could possibly imagine, in this classy, but cut-throat city.

c   Miranda and I caught the 9.45 train into the city, got off at Flinders Street, had a minor altercation with a rude ticket inspector, missed two trams but finally got the number 12 up to Princes Street where we met Joseph, Miranda's brother and Georgio, Joseph's friend, who took us to that groovy café in the Palladium Arcade, where someone saw Bono Vox, last time he was in Melbourne.

2   Rewrite these sentences, making them sound more interesting by altering their structure:

a   Evan was excited when he handed over his gift. _____

_____

b   We will miss the bus if we don't hurry. _____

_____

c   Aliyah turned over her final card and smiled sweetly. _____

_____

d   The soul of wit is brevity. _____

3   This text needs to be edited and made more effective. Rewrite it, making any changes you think necessary.

I always look forward to the school holidays. School holidays are much more fun than being at school. Usually on the school holidays my mum usually organises to do fun stuff. My mum takes us to the pool. She takes us to the movies. She takes us on bike rides. Sometimes my mum even takes us camping. These school holidays were not as good. My mum had to work. These school holidays we stayed at home and watched TV and stuff. It was okay though, just different. I liked being able to see as many DVDs as I liked.

Grammar
Unit 28
Double negatives

For those of you who are good at Maths, you will know that two negatives make a positive. This rule is also applicable to writing. Using the word *not* twice in one sentence produces a positive outcome and means you should not have used the word *not* in the first place:

I have finished my homework. (*positive statement*)   I have not finished my homework. (*negative statement*)

I haven't not finished my homework. (*two negative words equal a positive statement*)

Avoid **double negatives** and try to make positive statements rather than negative ones:

I am not unambitious. ✗   I am ambitious. ✓

It will not rain today. ✗   Today will be fine. ✓

1 Are these statements positive or negative?

a Unfortunately, the shop was not open. _____   d I was certain. _____

b Unfortunately, the shop was shut. _____   e I was not uncertain. _____

c I was uncertain. _____

2 Rewrite the following sentences, eliminating double negatives:

a It's not that Liu is not trying hard enough. _____

b If you weren't so aggressive, you wouldn't get in so much trouble. _____

_____

c The report didn't claim the politician wasn't corrupt. _____

_____

d Madeleine is not an unattractive girl. _____

3 Change these sentences so that they are written positively:

a My dog is not as poorly behaved as yours. _____

b Deepak's school didn't lack impressive sports facilities. _____

_____

c This novel has no real structure and no believable characters. _____

_____

4 Improve these sentences by altering or replacing some of the words:

a Your efforts this term have not been of a high standard, Finn. _____

_____

b 'Not talking to me is not going to help solve our problem, Hasan.' _____

_____

c I didn't see nobody. _____

d I didn't steal nothing. _____

e I do not want to accept your offer. _____

f It's not that I am untidy. _____

Grammar
Unit 29
More prefixes

Prefix	Meaning	Examples	Prefix	Meaning	Examples
'hyper'	over, above, more	hypertension, hyperinflation	'semi'	half	semicircle, semicolon
'in', 'im', 'il', 'ig', 'ir'	not	incorrect, impossible, illegal, ignoble, irrational	'sub'	under	submarine, subway
'mal'	ill, bad	malignant, malefactor	'super'	over	superhuman
'mis'	wrong	mislead, misspell	'tele'	far	telegram, telescope
'ob', 'op', 'o'	against	object, oppose	'trans'	across	transatlantic
'peri'	around	periscope, perimeter	'un'	not	unconscionable
'post'	after	postwar, postcode	'uni'	one	unicorn, unisex
're'	back, again	recycle, return			

1 Add one of the above prefixes to the following stems and then use the new word in a short sentence:

a _____ apprehension _____

b _____ ventilate _____

c _____ believable _____

d _____ power _____

2 Give three examples of words that use the following prefixes:

a 'poly' (many) _____

b 'syn', 'sym' (with) _____

c 'tri' (three) _____

d 'ultra' (beyond) _____

3 Add prefixes to two of the words in each of the following sentences to completely change their meaning:

a The principal was convinced by the students that the proposal was sound. _____

_____

b Unwar understood it was legal to use steroids six months before the national championships. _____

_____

c Dr Manning is a very sensitive and patient physician. _____

_____

4 Turn these words into their antonym by adding a prefix:

a caring _____

b movable _____

c lovable _____

d soluble _____

e resistible _____

f shockable _____

g material _____

h legitimate _____

i noble _____

Grammar
Unit 30
More suffixes

Prefix	Meaning	Examples	Prefix	Meaning	Examples
'fy'	to make	beautify, simplify	'ling'	little, or belonging to	duckling, earthling
'ic'	belonging or relating to	Icelandic, fantastic	'ly'	having the qualities of	cleverly, sisterly, studiously
'icle'	little	particle, icicle	'ous'	full of	copious, dangerous
'ion'	indicating action or condition	addition, temptation, radiation	'teen'	with the addition of ten	fifteen, thirteen
'ish'	having the nature of	outlandish, fiendish, childish, apish	'tude'	a condition of	attitude, aptitude
'ist'	one who	chemist, dentist	'ward'	indicating direction	homeward, westward
'less'	without	motherless, endless	'wise'	manner or way	clockwise, otherwise

1   Give examples of words that use the following suffixes:

a   'less' _____   c   'ist' _____

b   'ish' _____   d   'fy' _____

2   What suffixes can be added to these stem words? The first one has been done for you as an example.

a   beauty → beautiful, beautician, beautify, beautifully, beautification, beautifier

b   sad _____

c   inform _____

d   trim _____

e   act _____

3   State to which part of speech the following words belong. Then change each word's function by adding or removing a suffix and state the new word's part of speech. The first one has been done for you as an example:

a   mournfully → (adverb) → mourn → (verb)

b   immerse _____

c   oceanic _____

d   heavy _____

e   persecution _____

f   craftiest _____

g   volcano _____

h   harshly _____

i   sudden _____

j   demonic _____

Grammar
Unit 31
Using a dictionary revision

A **dictionary** is an essential tool for any writer. Whether you are doing homework, writing to Grandma, filling in a job application or just interested in what a word means, you need a good dictionary on your bookshelf.

How good are you at using a dictionary? Complete the following exercises to find out.

1 Number these words in the order you would find them in a dictionary:

a babe _____   f abhor _____   k baba _____

b babel _____   g bachelor _____   l baccalaureate _____

c abbot _____   h babble _____   m abdomen _____

d backchat _____   i abduct _____   n abacus _____

e abbess _____   j Bacchus _____

2 How long does it take you to find a word in the dictionary? Time yourself! Find the meanings of these words and record how long it took in the table:

Word	Meaning	Time
prose		
vermiform		
chapati		
tussock		
adroit		
omnipotent		
sprite		
hew		
dank		
vintner		

3 Answer the following questions:

a Where do the *Yuwaalaraay* people come from? _____

b Is the word *fugue* a musical or military term? _____

c Is the word *comprehensible* an adverb or adjective? _____

d What is the correct spelling of the word *cariccature*? _____

e Is a *humerus* a fungus or a bone? _____

f Was a *stegosaurus* a carnivore or a herbivore? _____

g Is a *hologram* three- or four-dimensional? _____

h Who uses a *pharos*? _____

i If somebody is *volatile*, are they likely to break out into laughter or violence? _____

j How many countries surround the *Black Sea*? _____

k If a missile is described as being *intercontinental*, how far can it travel? _____

Grammar

Grammar
Unit 32
Using a thesaurus revision

A **thesaurus** is an invaluable tool for finding synonyms to replace overused or humdrum words.

The first thing to do is to look up the word you wish to replace and carefully examine all the alternatives. When selecting a synonym, it is imperative that:

- you actually know what it means
- it is appropriate for the context (because some synonyms sound fabulous but may not be suitable for your particular sentence) and
- it is from the same part of speech as your original word (you cannot, for example, replace an adjective with an adverb).

1 Find a synonym for each of these words:

a folly _____

b overwrought _____

c youthful _____

d bewitch _____

e ostracise _____

f scourge _____

2 Replace the italicised words in the exercises below with the appropriate synonym from this list: *abhor, animosity, counterfeit, forged, hefty, infuriated, portent, reasonable.*

a Experts declared the painting was a *copy*. _____

b I *hate* maggots. _____

c Henrik's *massive* muscles came in handy. _____

d It's a *sound* and interesting idea. _____

e Christy *faked* her Dad's signature. _____

f War is often the result of *hatred*. _____

g Gerald's insults left Monica *indignant*. _____

h Hilda felt the arrival of the raven was an *omen*. _____

3 Rewrite this advertisement, making it more effective by using a thesaurus to replace the italicised words with better, more interesting ones (but keep in mind the purpose of an advertisement):

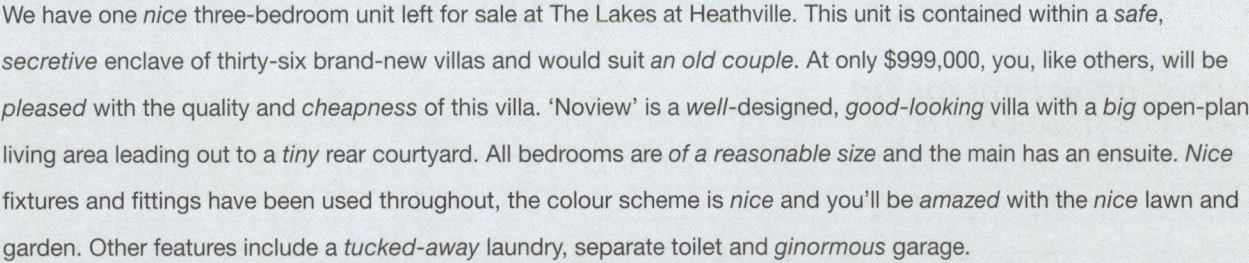

We have one *nice* three-bedroom unit left for sale at The Lakes at Heathville. This unit is contained within a *safe*, *secretive* enclave of thirty-six brand-new villas and would suit *an old couple*. At only $999,000, you, like others, will be *pleased* with the quality and *cheapness* of this villa. 'Noview' is a *well*-designed, *good-looking* villa with a *big* open-plan living area leading out to a *tiny* rear courtyard. All bedrooms are *of a reasonable size* and the main has an ensuite. *Nice* fixtures and fittings have been used throughout, the colour scheme is *nice* and you'll be *amazed* with the *nice* lawn and garden. Other features include a *tucked-away* laundry, separate toilet and *ginormous* garage.

If you are looking for a quiet, *boring* lifestyle, surrounded by *other oldies*, then 'Noview' villa is for you. Call The No Imagination Real Estate Agency NOW on 1300 999 875 for a *pressure*-free inspection. Don't *hang around thinking about it though*; this is a *good* opportunity you shouldn't miss.

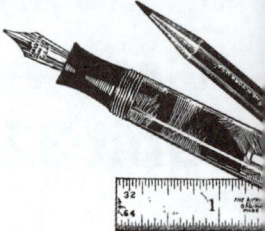

Imagine that you are completing work experience with a city sign writer. One of your tasks is to vet the signs before they are painted. You quickly realise how important your job is! Rewrite the following signs.

Its time for a bright change: free environmental-friendly light-bulbs (subject to availability.)

20% of childrens shoes
25% of selected mens' wear
30% of all homeware's

Have you returned your tray!

NO UNDER-18s ALOUD

Fifi's flower's
Beautiful cut flower's at reasonable price's.
Delivered to your loved ones door.

The consumption of alcohol are not permitted on these premise

SOPHOCLES SOCK SHOP

Mr. Money Make a appointment with myself for financial advise.

Relive the 60's, retro dance night Feb 17th at the palais theatre.

DANGER!! ENTER AT YOU'RE OWN RISK!!

BRISBANE BAPTIST LADIES COLLAGE

TOMATOS AND POTATOS FOR SAIL.
$10 A BOX OR $17 FOR TWO BOXS

major mitchell memorial 500 metres

Should you of replaced youre old tyres?
Drop into Teds Tyres for an free safety check.

YOU TO CAN TAKE PHOTO'S LIKE THESE! COMPLETE
ONE OFF OUR SHORT COURSE AND IN THREE WEEKS,
YOULL BE TAKING SHOTS LIKE A PRO!!!

Grammar
Unit 34
Final revision 2

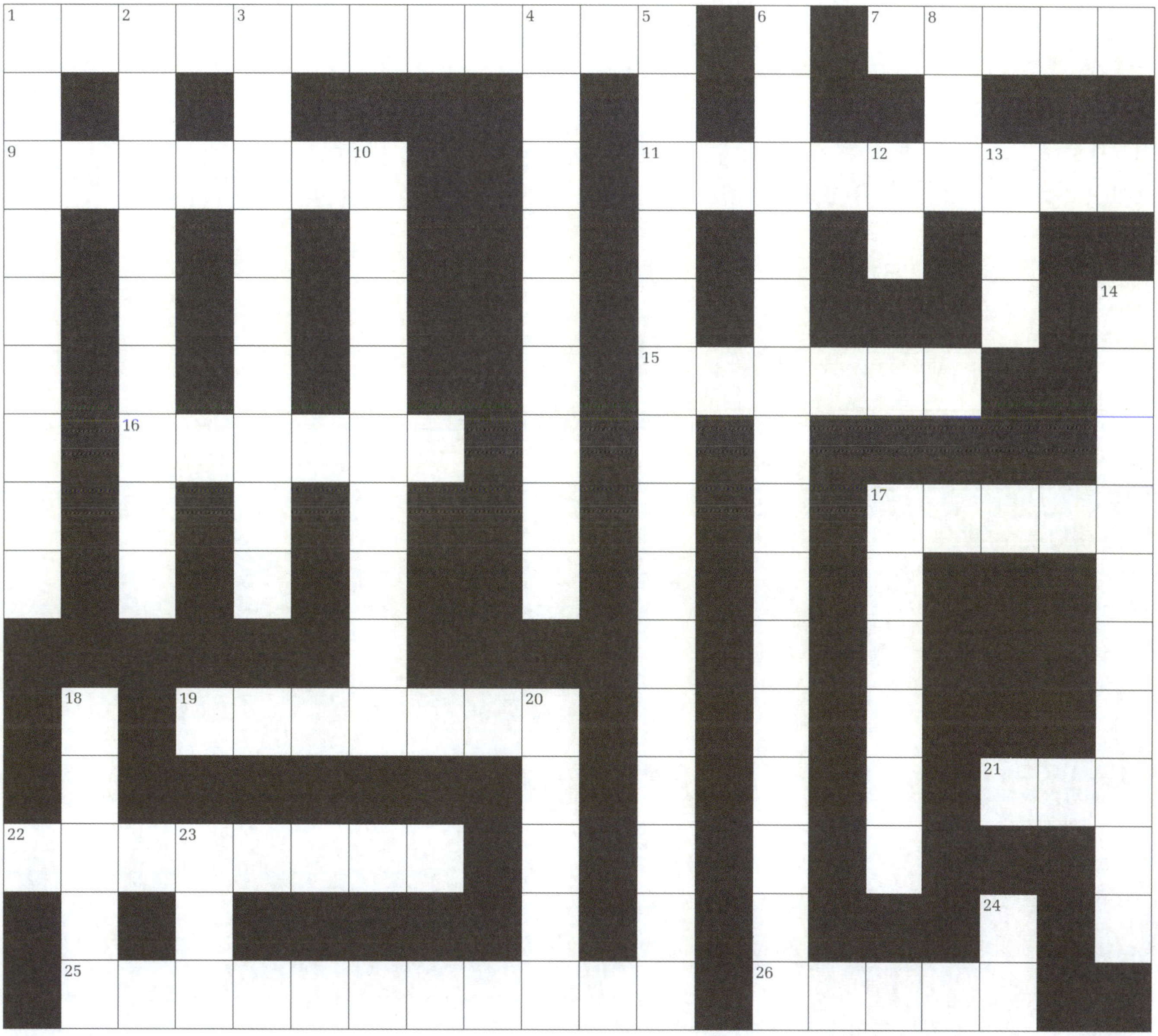

Across

1 Adjectival form of *catastrophe*
7 Punctuation mark used to introduce long lists
9 Synonym of *accomplice*
11 Synonym of *profitable*
15 The largest group of nouns
16 Past tense of *rain*
17 Antonym of *sharp*
19 Part of speech that modifies verbs
21 Article with three letters
22 Words that have more than one meaning
25 Another name for *brackets*
26 Third person singular of the verb *to know* in the present tense

Down

1 Synonym of *lunacy*
2 Dictionary of *synonyms*
3 First person singular of the verb *to satisfy* in the past tense
4 Adverbial form of *hurry*
5 Words that name groups of people, animals and things
6 Punctuation mark at the end of exclamatory sentences
8 Antonym of *in*
10 Pronouns that refer back to the subject
12 The article that precedes words beginning with a vowel
13 Third person possessive pronoun
14 Homophone of *stationary*
17 The correct spelling of the verb *bemews*
18 Singular form of the noun *sloops*
20 Plural form of *sift*
23 First person plural possessive pronoun
24 Third person singular of the verb *to be* in the present tense

Amanda Ford
Elizabeth Haywood
Judy Conlan
Marie Henley

Part 2
Spelling

As well as consolidating and improving spelling skills, this section will help students to build their vocabularies and make them more aware of the dynamic nature of language. To this end, the 34 units have been injected with humour wherever possible to avoid the tedium which can accompany this type of skills work.

This section includes traditional activities as well as more creative exercises. Vocabulary items reappear in spelling lists, instructions and exercises so that students become increasingly confident about both using and spelling these words correctly.

Most activities are to be completed in the book which provides plenty of space for answers; activities marked by the icon can be done off the page and are ideal for extension work in class or at home.

Spelling
Unit 1
How not to say what you mean

A **euphemism** is a mild expression used in place of a harsh or blunt one; for example, *deceased* instead of *dead*. Student report cards often contain euphemisms.

admit   assignment   concentration 集中   daub 乱画,涂抹   debris 残渣   despite √轻视/蔑视   disintegrating 下解的
disrupting 分裂   distinct 独特的   excursions   experiments   grammar   illiterate 文盲   inaccurate 不准确的
labelled 贴上标签   laboratory 实验室   menace n. 胁迫   odour 气味   opportunity 机会   prime   spatial 空间的
specimens 样本   V. 威胁   n. 全盛时期
                                                                    adj 首要的
                                                                    v. 使准备好

1 Here is an extract from Jane's report card, and below it is a true statement of what the teacher really meant by each remark. Supply appropriate forms of words from the word list to fill in the blanks:

English   Jane needs help at home to improve her g **rammer** r. Her c **oncentration** n is poor.

Science   Jane needs to take more care with her chemistry e **xperiment** ts. Zoology _____ are poorly marked and stored.

History   Jane tries very hard and shows some interest.

Geography Jane's work might improve if she had a textbook in class. Her work is generally untidy.

- - - - - - - - - -

English   I ___**admit**___ defeat. *You* try to teach this il **literate** te girl. Jane is a m **enace** e in the classroom, dis **rupting** lessons at every **opportunity**.

Science   The l **aboratory** y is still here, despite Jane's many attempts to blow it up. Flies are l **abelled** d caterpillars and there are d **isintegrating** g moths and other d **ebris** s all over the classroom floor.

History   Despite the fact that Jane thinks that Captain Cook is the P **rime** e Minister of Australia, she is at least making an effort.

Geography Jane spends most of her lesson doing field work in the form of e **xcursions** ns to the playground where she hopes to find her textbooks. Yesterday, there was a **odour** smell of Weetbix on one page of her a **ssignment** t and a d _____ b of honey on the other.

2 What are the 'real' meanings of these euphemisms?

a between jobs _____   d it fell off the back of a truck _____

b broad in the beam _____   e tired and emotional _____

c dropped off the perch _____

3 Write two reports on your own English (or mathematical) skills.

- One report is to be written from the point of view of your teacher; the other from your own point of view.
- The teacher's report will contain euphemisms; your own report will be brutally honest.

Spelling
Unit 2
A challenge

1 Replace the word or phrase in italics with a word of similar meaning from the word list:

a The political candidate was *sarcastically* criticised by his opponent. _____

b The beggar was *bereft* of clothing and dignity. _____

c The boy who had been struck by his classmate *repaid the insult*. _____

d Gangs of lawless youths have been known to commit *wanton* murder of innocent strangers. _____

e The *loathsome* child was terrorising the gentle old lady by persistently ringing her doorbell. _____

f *Thrifty* housekeeping enabled the pensioner to save for a holiday. _____

g The thief *stealthily* approached the building, taking care to use the cover of the trees. _____

h As the student was constantly *aggressive*, his parents were asked to remove him from the school. _____

i Aware of the complexity of the problem, the *shrewd* politician was careful not to commit herself. _____

j In a *shrill* voice, the interjector at the political rally contradicted the speaker. _____

2 Find words in the word list to match these meanings:

a in high spirits _____   **e** spur _____

b to give up _____   **f** tiresome _____

c to force _____   **g** secluded _____

d to hold back _____

3 Find four synonyms for the word *duress*:

_____   _____

_____   _____

4 Draw coloured lines to match these words with their antonyms:

a strident   peaceful

b furtive   exciting

c tedious   lavish

d frugal   soft

e belligerent   unconcealed

5 Write a report, from the point of view of a teacher, about an incident in the schoolyard. Include the following words from the word list: *unprovoked, incite, belligerent, retaliated, restrain.*

6 Now write another report of the incident from Exercise 5, this time from the point of view of one of the students involved.

Spelling
Unit 3
Super deals for super fools

There is a special language for advertising, often relying on **hyperbole** (extravagant statements not to be taken literally). A house may be described as having 'unsurpassed ocean views', for example, when there is really only a glimpse of the sea from the roof!

advertisement	allotment	ambition	conformity	derelict	envy	fear
greed	inferior	instinct	intellectual status	investment	landscaped	magnificent
maternal	pity	pride	purchase	quaint	refreshing	romance
snobbery	social status	statistics	vanity	instinct		

1 Examine these advertisements, then supply words from the word list to fill in the spaces:

a Do you wake up like a grizzly bear after a night tossing on an _____ mattress? A

Dreammaster fabulous inner-sprung, divan-type bed is the answer. Durable fabric covers. An _____,

not a purchase.

b Sell: _____ cottage on superb _____ near sea. Magnificent

ocean views. _____ gardens. Attractive setting. $525,000 o.n.o. Ph. 92876431.

2 Find synonyms from the word list for:

a data _____   **c** conceit _____   **e** motherly _____

b ruined _____   **d** avarice _____   **f** jealousy _____

3 Use suitable forms of the words in italics to complete the following:

a *conformity:* _____ to the rules   **d** *investment:* _____ interest

b *statistics:* _____ evidence   **e** *romance:* _____ setting

c *inferior:* _____ complex   **f** *derelict:* _____ of duty

4 Use the words *allot* and *a lot* in sentences which show their meaning. _____

_____

_____

_____

5 The following advertisements are examples of the use of hyperbole in advertising. To what does each one appeal? (Use the word list for ideas.) How much fact or opinion do they express? Discuss with a partner.

a Mrs Corney's custard pies taste best.

b Statistics prove that ninety-eight per cent of men prefer Stunner hair oil.

c Roof Cure will mend your roof more cheaply. Ten-year guarantee.

d Nine out of ten astronauts recommend Boom rocket fuel.

6 Write your own advertising copy for a new product, perhaps a new computer game or car. Make use of hyperbole!

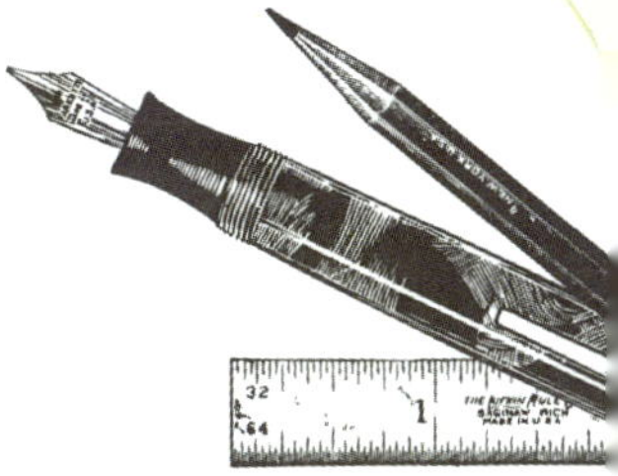

Spelling
Unit 4
Take care!

The words in this list are 'spelling demons'. They are often spelt incorrectly. The word *mischievous*, for example, is often mistakenly spelt *mischievious*.

accommodation	alcohol	coming	conscious	criticism	definite	embarrass
environment	existence	February	government	interruption	loneliness	medicine
mischievous	necessity	parallel	parliament	possession	recommend	refrigerator
remember	rhyme	rhythm	schedule	scraping	scrapped	separate
surprise	temporary	theory	vehicle			

1 Find words from the word list that match the following words and phrases:

- a timetable ____________
- b aware ____________
- c disapproval ____________
- d rasping ____________
- e need ____________
- f belittle ____________
- g isolation ____________
- h naughty ____________
- i supposition ____________
- j lines that never meet are ____________
- k seat of government ____________
- l opposite of permanent ____________
- m used to treat illness ____________
- n a break in the continuity ____________
- o removed from use ____________
- p surrounding conditions ____________
- q approaching ____________
- r suggest ____________
- s disconnected ____________
- t life ____________
- u absolute ____________
- v beat ____________
- w recollect ____________
- x ownership ____________
- y living quarters ____________
- z carriage or conveyance ____________
- aa month following January ____________
- bb repetition of sound ____________
- cc unexpected occurrence ____________
- dd ruling body ____________
- ee intoxicant present in beer, wine, etc. ____________
- ff cabinet designed for cold storage ____________

2
- a Find two words from the word list with a silent 'n': ____________
- b Find two words from the word list which end in 'ous': ____________
- c What are the first two months of the year? ____________

3 Provide words from the word list, or appropriate forms of them, that could be used with these words or phrases:

- a ____________ conditions
- b constructive ____________
- c ____________ to the coast
- d ____________ stupor
- e swaying to the ____________
- f ____________ by the suggestion
- g ____________ of terms
- h ____________ of his error
- i ____________ the sheep from the goats
- j ____________ for mercy
- k ____________ incapacitated
- l ____________ is nine-tenths of the law
- m it is not ____________
- n ____________ prank

4 Run a spelling bee in class, using the words from the word list.

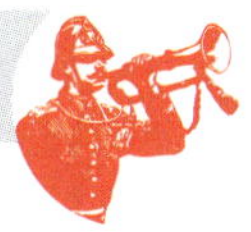

Spelling

Choose a word circle. Working in pairs, make up a list of twenty questions based on the activities used in these units. For example:

a Spell the word _____

b Give a synonym/antonym for _____

c Form a descriptive word from _____

Use your questions to test the rest of your class.

foundation
assertion
demonstration
justification   exhibition
convention   civilisation
association   imitation
realisation   reflection   ignition
expedition   recognition
edition   definition
superstition

angrily
guiltily   easily   hungrily   centrally
gaily   sleepily   eerily   warily   stealthily   skilfully
basically   completely   really   truly   frantically   comically
tragically   hurriedly   publicly   generally   occasionally   practically
courageously   gradually   obviously   evidently   awkwardly
tragically   periodically

available
reasonable   capable   admirable
comfortable   suitable   irritable   inflammable   innumerable
imaginable   memorable   dependable   vulnerable   impressionable
creditable   honourable   advisable   uncontrollable   manageable
irreplaceable   noticeable   changeable   serviceable
agreeable

past
passed   moral
morale   chose   choose
uninterested   disinterested
principal   principle   imminent
eminent   picture   alternative
pitcher   alternate   personnel
illegible   personal   eligible
bought
brought

repentant
triumphant   relevant
incessant   abundant
reluctant   tolerant   resultant
flagrant   immigrant   hesitant
repentant   significant   valiant
arrogant   consultant
occupant
defendant   remnant

quarrelled
tunnelled   controlled
travelled   worshipped
permitted   admitted   committed
forgotten   forbidden   enrolled
repelled   propelled   compelled
cancelled   transferred   referred
deferred   concurred   conferred
occurred
recurred

potential   substantial
torrential   confidential
initial   influential   preferential
partial   beneficial   artificial
controversial   commercial

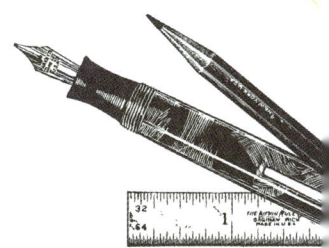

Spelling
Unit 6
Say what you mean

acceptable	amiable	apprehensive	appropriate	bigoted	congenial	conscientious
delectable	eccentric	equitable	exciting	extravagant	indiscreet	invigorating
irreproachable	luxurious	pleasant	satisfying	startled	timid	valuable

1 Replace the words *really great* in each of the following sentences with a more precise word from the word list:

a My friend's house is really great because it has a billiard room and an indoor swimming pool, as well as spacious rooms and antique furniture. _____

b The dinner my mother served at the party was really great. _____

c Although Jane is generally a really great person, she is sometimes spiteful and rude. _____

d Most people like to picnic in really great surroundings where they feel relaxed. _____

e Climbing the mountain was a really great adventure. _____

2 Replace the word *stupid* in each of the following sentences:

a You must be stupid if you think that one race is more intelligent than another. _____

b How can you insist that you are not stupid when you eat ice cream in the bath? _____

c Telling Joan that you don't like her brother was stupid. _____

d A gold pair of shoes is a stupid gift to give a friend. _____

3 Replace the word *good* in each of the following sentences:

a I think *In Defence of the Citizen* is a good title for the book. _____

b The students had a good holiday skiing in New Zealand. _____

c When called to give evidence at the trial, the clergyman claimed that the accused's character was good. _____

4 Replace the word *good* in each of the following phrases:

a good student _____

b good watch _____

c good law _____

d good arrangement _____

e good meal _____

5 Which words in the word list can be used to mean *frightened*? _____

_____

6 In groups, brainstorm words which are more precise than the following (choose one word for each group): *nice, cool, fantastic, big, small, fabulous, awesome.* Use each word you come up with in a sentence which shows its exact meaning.

7 You are a super salesperson who can sell anything to anyone. Write the argument you would use if you wanted to sell a skeleton of a sheep to a musician, or any other useless item to an unlikely buyer. Present your argument to the class.

Spelling
Unit 7
Reach for the stars

The Latin suffix 'al' means 'relating to'. *Educational*, for example, relates to *education*.

camouflage	capacity	confiscate	conventional	dedicate	desolation	devastation
devotion	dilapidated	discipline	dynamite	educational	enclosure	enervated
eucalyptus	isolation	instructive	meteor	satellite	surrender	

1 Form adjectives ending with 'al' from the following words:

a devotion ___ ~~deve~~ *devotional* ___   c instruction *instructional* ___

b benefit *beneficial* ___   d accident *accidental* ___

2 Complete these sentences:

a Dynamite unleashes energy in the form of an explosion; a *dynamic* ___ person is one who is very energetic.

b A meteor is a shooting star; a *meteoric* ___ rise to fame is ~~a~~ ~~as –supp dulen~~ ~~ ~~ *prise to fame*

c A satellite is an artificial body launched from and encircling the earth; a *satellite* ___ town is

3 You all know what *discipline* is! What is the name given to a person who believes in the strict maintenance of discipline?

___

4 Explain the difference between *energetic* and *enervated*. ___

___

___

5 Use these words in sentences in the context indicated:

a devote (time) ___

b convention (meeting) ___

c capacity (crowd) ___

d isolate (disease) ___

e dedication (study) ___

6 Match each word with a synonym from the word list:

a instructive ___   e secluded ___   h disguise ___

b seize ___   f punitive ___   i dedication ___

c customary ___   g compound ___   j decrepit ___

d submit ___

7 Imagine you are in charge of an army unit sent to retrieve a satellite that has crashed in the outback. Write a paragraph describing the scene, using as many words as possible from the word list.

Spelling

Spelling
Unit 8
Technology rules!

- The prefix 'inter' comes from Latin and means 'between or among'. *International* means 'between nations'.
- The prefix 'multi' comes from Latin, meaning 'more than one'. *Multinational* means 'many nations'.

access	circuit	digital	encryption	integrated	interactive	interfere
interject	international	internet	interplay	interstate	interview	media
memory	multimedia	network	pixel	reception	wireless	

1 Give the meanings of the following 'inter' words:

a interstate _____

b internet _____

c interject _____

d interview _____

e interfere _____

2 a Give the meaning of *multimedia*. _____

b Find two more words with the prefix 'multi' and give their meanings. _____

_____

_____

3 Complete these sentences, using appropriate forms of words from the word list:

a The _____ provides more information than we can process.

b Some programs use _____ to prevent hackers from stealing information.

c Mobile phones can have poor _____ in the hills.

d Cameras generally have clearer photos if they have more _____.

e Cables are not needed if you have _____ internet.

4 Words relating to technology often have other, earlier meanings. *Boot* can mean 'footwear' as well as the starting of your computer. Give the non-technological meaning of the following:

a reception _____

b desktop _____

c mouse _____

d bookmark _____

e icon _____

f scan _____

g access _____

h memory _____

5 New words are being created every day. Create a display of recent words relating to the world of technology.

Spelling
Unit 9
Our affluent society

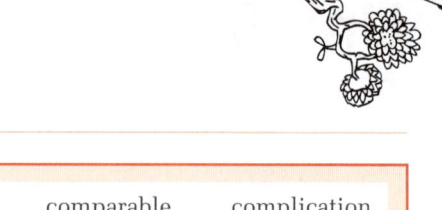

acquisitive	affluent	applicable	beneficial	calculate	comparable	complication
conversational	desperation	development	excitable	exclamation	explanatory	necessitate
obligatory	persuasion	preparatory	prosperity	relevant	repetitive	

1 Find antonyms for the following:

a benefit _____

b comparable _____

c complicate _____

d prosper _____

e relevant _____

f inflation _____

2 Complete this table (the first has been done for you as an example):

Verb	Adjective	Noun
prosper	prosperous	prosperity
necessitate		
		obligation
		beneficiary
	explanatory	
		comparison
	applicable	
		desperation

3 Find appropriate forms of words from the word list that are synonyms for:

a profitable _____

b relevant _____

c procure _____

d similar _____

e volatile _____

f affluent _____

g compulsory _____

4 Draw coloured lines to match these sentence halves:

a The development of the housing project — relevant to the argument.

b That rule is not — I presumed he was speaking to a friend.

c Man's acquisitive nature — was delayed by floods

d Judging by the conversational tone of his voice, — is debated by some educationalists.

e The necessity of examinations — applicable in this situation.

f That comment is hardly — causes unnecessary depletion of our resources.

5 Write a speech (or hold a debate) on the topic 'It is better to give than to receive', pointing out the dangers of affluence.

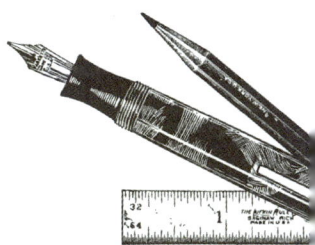

confined	divulging	dreaded	effective	execution	fate	fiendish
humanely	inevitably	infamous	infested	instruments	melancholy	merciful
occupant	refuge	severity	sinister	solitary	tormentors	

1 Fill in the blanks using words from the word list:

The Tower of London has a m _____ y history of imprisonment and torture. While it is true that most prisoners

were treated _____, some were _____ in the infamous 'Dungeon of the rats', so called

because, at high tide, it became _____ with rats seeking _____ from the water. There was an

even more s _____ r fate for others, a prison so small that its _____ o _____ t

could neither stand nor move. The two most dreaded _____ were the rack and the Scavenger's

Daughter. The former, which stretched the body, was effective as its _____ could be controlled;

the latter, which crushed the body, was even more f _____ sh. If a person survived these tortures

without _____ his secrets, the _____ that _____ followed was merciful.

2 Highlight the word from the bracketed list that is closest in meaning to the italicised word, as it is used in the passage:

a *confined* (hidden, imprisoned, tied, placed)

b *divulge* (reveal, confess, admit, recite)

c *dreaded* (detested, loathed, despised, feared)

d *humanely* (generously, humanly, affectionately, compassionately)

e inevitably (unavoidably, invincibly, undoubtedly, unfortunately)

f *infamous* (awesome, obscure, abominable, dark)

g *melancholy* (weird, gloomy, disappointing, ruthless)

h *refuge* (help, consolation, salvation, shelter)

i *sinister* (serious, sure, unexpected, fiendish)

3 a Write sentences to show you know the meanings of *effect* and *affect*. Make sure you use *effect* both as a verb and as a noun.

_____

_____

_____

b What does *ineffective* mean? _____

_____

4 Find out the origin and meaning of the word *incarcerate*.

5 Write a story in which you travel back in time to the Middle Ages in England. Describe how it is that you came to time travel and what you find when you arrive in the past. Use as many words from the word list as possible and highlight each one you use.

Spelling

Spelling
Unit 11
'ious' and 'uous' suffixes

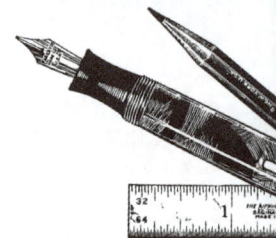

> * The suffixes 'ious' and 'uous' form adjectives meaning 'full of, characterised by'. The noun *religion* becomes the adjective *religious*, for example.
> * The 'shush' sound of the 'ious' endings of the words in the second list is usually created because it follows a 'c' or a 't'.

arduous	continuous	impetuous	inconspicuous	innocuous	virtuous
strenuous	tenuous				

conscientious	contagious	delicious	gracious	judicious	luscious
malicious	ostentatious	precocious	pretentious	religious	spacious
suspicious	unconscious	vicious			

1 Match these words with adjectives from the first word list:

a _____ blemish   **d** _____ action   **g** _____ task

b _____ act   **e** _____ argument   **h** _____ remark

c _____ exercise   **f** _____ winds

2 Form adverbs from words in the second word list to match these verbs (for example, *replied virtuously*):

a lurking _____   **d** praying _____

b accepted _____   **e** lying _____

c attacked _____

3 Find synonyms from the word lists for:

a rash _____   **e** uninterrupted _____

b roomy _____   **f** infectious _____

c ostentatious _____   **g** laborious _____

d spiteful _____

4 Use *continuous* and *continual* in sentences to show the difference in meaning. _____

_____

_____

5 Complete each sentence using the appropriate form of words from the word lists:

a The _____ verbal attack on him by the stranger left him speechless.

b Surrounded by _____ grounds, the residence stood majestically on the headland.

c _____ children are never popular when they dominate conversations.

d _____ of the insult, she babbled on happily.

e Special care should be taken to isolate children from _____ diseases like hepatitis.

6 Use five of the words in the word lists in a paragraph about heli-skiing or abseiling.

Spelling
Unit 12
'ible' suffixes

The suffix 'ible' is a variant of the suffix 'able'. These suffixes are used to form adjectives, especially from verbs, to denote *ability*, *tendency* or *likelihood*; for example, permission → permissible.

accessible	compatible	contemptible	convertible	discernible	fallible
feasible	incomprehensible	incredible	indelible	inexhaustible	invincible
invisible	irrepressible	irresistible	negligible	permissible	plausible
responsible	susceptible				

Spelling

1 Choose a word from the word list that means:

a credible _____

b liable to error _____

c impossible to conquer _____

d deserving scorn _____

e can be changed _____

f unintelligible _____

g infinite _____

h possible _____

i harmonious, well matched _____

j allowed _____

k insignificant _____

l trustworthy _____

m visible _____

n cannot be restrained _____

o possible to reach _____

p that cannot be seen _____

2 Make these words opposite in meaning by adding a prefix:

a _____ responsible

b _____ credible

c _____ exhaustible

d _____ compatible

e _____ fallible

f _____ accessible

g _____ comprehensible

h _____ discernible

3 Give the verb from which the following adjectives have been formed:

a accessible _____

b responsible _____

c convertible _____

4 Choose appropriate forms of words from the word list to complete these sentences:

a Her sense of humour was quite _____.

b Study has shown that this proposal is quite _____.

c During the season, the football team became renowned for its _____ back line.

d Unfortunately, its forwards were not _____, as the goal scores testified.

e Such _____ damage hardly warrants such concern.

f The mountain hideaway was completely _____ except by helicopter.

g The partners were so _____ that the only solution was to dissolve their business agreement.

h The wearing of jewellery with school uniforms is usually not _____.

5 Devise a spelling test list of 10 'ible' words and 10 'able' words. Then, in pairs, conduct your tests orally.

Spelling
Unit 13
Watch your step

abundance	aridity	conversion	doubtful	enmity	exemplary	exemplify
independence	inseparable	irregularity	knowledgeable	leisure	lucid	opaque
psychologist	relevancy	stomach	transparency	vigilance	vivacious	

1 One word is wrongly included in each of the following groups. Highlight it:

a leisure, deceit, distinctly, receipt

b vivacious, precious, vicious, tortuous, precocious

c spinster, actress, goddess, heiress

d ignorance, maintenance, abundance, assurance, independence

e shoulder, wrist, stomach, knee, tongue, fetlock

f knitted, gnawed, psychologist, knowledge, grovel, doubtful

g irresistible, susceptible, incredible, contemptible, convertible, adaptable

h irrepressible, irresponsible, irregular, irrelevant, inseparable

i envious, lucid, opaque, arid, transparent

j awkwardly, absurdly, exemplary, ideally, vigilantly

2 Where possible, perform each of the following tasks on the corresponding groups of words in Exercise 1:

a Change the words to adjectives. _____

b Pair each word with a noun to show its meaning. _____
_____

c Change the words to the opposite gender. _____

d Change the words to adverbs. _____

e Pair each word with another word beginning with the same letter; for example, *tongue-tied*. _____
_____

f Change nouns to adjectives, adjectives to nouns and find synonyms for the other words. _____
_____

g Pair each word with a noun to show its meaning. _____
_____

h Write an antonym for each word. _____

i Pair each word with a noun that shows its meaning. _____
_____

j Change the words to adjectives. _____
_____

3 Explain the difference between *exemplary* and *exemplify* to a classmate.

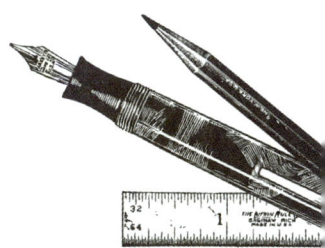

Spelling
Unit 14
Suffixes, suffixes, suffixes

'ent':	allotment	deterrent	enrolment	equipment	fulfilment
'ion':	cancellation	compulsion	expulsion	repulsion	permission
'ence':	emergence	impudence	inference	malevolence	occurrence
	preference	prevalence	reference	resilience	transference
'ance':	admittance				

1 Complete this table (the first one has been done for you as an example):

Verb	Adjective	Noun
prefer	preferred	preference
	deterred	
		inference
	transferred	
allot		
		occurrence
	enrolled	
equip		
		fulfilment

2 Expand these word groups to make your own sentences:

a allotment of shares: _____

b deterrent to crime: _____

c admittance to the gymnasium: _____

d faulty equipment: _____

e fulfilment of a dream: _____

f the cancellation of the concert: _____

g occurred spontaneously: _____

h referral to a specialist: _____

3 Form verbs from the words in the word list that could be used in these phrases (for example, 'occurred at night'):

a _____ from the school

b _____ by the smoke

c _____ with breathing apparatus

d _____ to a new school

e _____ that I was wrong

f _____ in the course

g _____ from the forest

h _____ to enter

4 a Explain the difference between *repulsion*, *compulsion* and *expulsion*.

b Find the Latin derivation common to all three words.

Spelling
Unit 15
Use your senses

Hearing:	clanging	discordant	metallic	raucous	screech	shrill	squeal	wail
Sight:	awesome	distorted	grotesque	gruesome				
Touch:	abrasive	bristling	jagged	taut	tepid			
Taste:	candied	savoury	succulent	tart				
Smell:	aromatic	musty	pungent	putrid				

1 Choose words from the word list to describe:

a the feel of:

   i a baby's bath water _____

   ii wet tent ropes _____

   iii whiskers _____

   iv sandpaper _____

b the taste of:

   i lemon juice _____

   ii honeycomb _____

   iii sausage rolls _____

c the smell of:

   i spices _____

   ii burning rubber _____

   iii a room closed for a long period _____

   iv rotting animals or decaying vegetation _____

d the sight of:

   i yourself when viewed in a concave mirror in a fun park _____

   ii a Halloween mask _____

   iv gargoyles _____

   iii a daring trapeze act with no net _____

e the sound of:

   i brakes applied to car wheels _____

   ii geese cackling _____

   iii a spoon dropping onto a stainless steel sink _____

   iv the blast of a whistle _____

   v an old man's voice _____

2 Find synonyms in the word list for:

a acrid _____

b harsh _____

c acidic _____

d warm _____

e juicy _____

f misshapen _____

3 Using some words from the word list, as well as words of your own, write a sentence about each of the following:

- the noise of a motorbike
- the smell of a bakery
- the feel of a fish

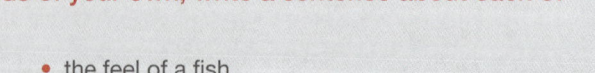

4 Have a class discussion on the topic: Which of the five senses is most important to you?

Spelling
Unit 16
Your horoscope

机会主义者   短暂的

1 The prefix 'astro' is derived from the Greek word for *star*. Give the meaning of the following 'astro' words:

a astronomy _____

b astrology _____

c astrobiology _____

d astrophysics _____

e astronaut _____

2 Some people believe implicitly in astrology; others think it is utter nonsense! For fun, look at your star sign's characteristics (if you don't know your star sign, check the newspaper). Notice that all the qualities listed are positive ones. See if you can rewrite the list in a cynical manner (that is, showing negative qualities). The first one has been done for you as an example:

a *Aries*: adventurous, ambitious → willing to do anything, irresponsible, opportunist

b *Libra*: romantic, artistic _____

c *Taurus*: dependable, practical _____

d *Scorpio*: courageous, magnetic _____

e *Gemini*: versatile, restless, charming _____

f *Sagittarius*: optimistic, adventurous _____

g *Cancer*: sensitive, protective _____

h *Capricorn*: conscientious, tireless _____

i *Leo*: affectionate, enterprising, vain _____

j *Aquarius*: self-contained, unconventional _____

k *Virgo*: practical, perfectionist _____

l *Pisces*: sensitive, versatile _____

3 Complete these sentence fragments:

a To predict the outcome _____

b It was such an auspicious occasion _____

c I had believed implicitly in _____

d So disturbing was the news _____

4 Write a letter to a magazine complaining about their astrology page.

Spelling

Spelling
Unit 17
Practice makes perfect

aggravate	automation	autumnal	basically	enervate	hostility	humorous
hungrily	intrepid	liveliest 最难记的 loneliness		monumental	pensive	remedial
replies	stoppage	supplicate	symmetry	utterance	vicinity	

1 Use a word from the word list to complete these sentences:

a _____ is a noun from *hostile*.

b _____ implies *balance*.

c _____ is a noun from *lonely*.

d _____ is an adjective from *remedy*.

e _____ is a noun from *stop*.

f _____ is the 3rd person singular of *reply*.

g _____ means *neighbourhood*.

h _____ means *to weaken*.

i _____ means *thoughtful*.

j _____ is a noun from *automatic*.

k _____ is an adjective from *monument*.

l _____ is an adverb from *hunger*.

m _____ is an adverb from *basic*.

n _____ is an adjective from *autumn*.

o _____ is the adjective from *humour*.

p _____ is the superlative degree of *lively*.

q _____ means *to make worse*.

r _____ is a noun from *utter*.

s _____ means *beg*.

t _____ means *dauntless or fearless*.

2 Use these phrases in sentences:

a to aggravate the problem: _____

_____

b the symmetry of the vase: _____

_____

c in the vicinity: _____

_____

d political utterance: _____

_____

e pensive mood: _____

_____

3 Use a form of the words in italics in the blank spaces:

a *loneliness*: the _____ traveller

b *hostility*: _____ neighbours

c *automation*: _____ reaction

d *humorous*: grim _____

e *utterance*: _____ a few syllables

f *supplicate*: humble _____

g *remedial*: _____ the situation

4 Write a newspaper report about an intrepid traveller returning from a long voyage.

Spelling
Unit 18
Singapore stopover

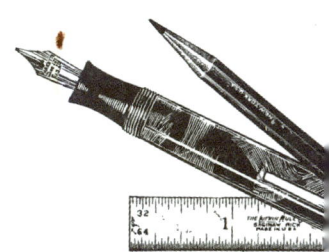

accommodation	airport	attendant	baggage	brochures	cancellation	currency
declaration	departure	destination	documents	estimated	excess	inspected
itinerary	label	proportion	reservation	temporary	tourism	vaccinations
valuables	visa					

1 Use words from the word list, or appropriate forms of them, to fill in the blanks:

Not included in your stopover: Passport, laundry, _____ (cholera, typhoid, and yellow fever), expenses en route, insurance, meals, extra tours, medical expenses, _____ baggage.

Cancellations: If the _____ is made one month prior to the date of your _____ a small fee will be charged. If you cancel after this date, you may incur a much higher fee.

Booking: To make a _____, please advise your travel agent of the length of time you plan to stay in Singapore. He/she will plan your _____, arrange temporary _____ at a hotel, advise about foreign _____, and help you secure the many _____ you need before your departure.

Baggage: _____ all cases clearly. Leave your _____ at home.

Note: Your _____ time of arrival is not always your actual time of arrival. When you reach your _____ you will be required to make a customs _____ before you are allowed to leave the international _____. Your flight _____ will help you fill out the form. Your passport will be _____.

Sightseeing: Ask to see our many _____, which show you the main sights in Singapore.

2 One word (or a form of it) from the word list can be used in all three of these sentences. Find it:

a Until Joe was caught stealing I always believed him to be honourable but now I have some _____ about his integrity.

b As I was making stock, I decided to _____ some to use later.

c Supplies of petrol were held in _____ for emergency use.

3 Draw coloured lines to match these words with their synonyms:

a vaccinate   revoke

b baggage   exorbitant

c excessive   schedule

d cancel   money

e currency   inoculate

f itinerary   luggage

4 Write a travel diary entry about your Singapore (or other country) stopover.

abundant	accomplished	acknowledge 承认	adjacent	advocate 提出的	allocation	assert
assurance	campaign	criticism 批评	delinquent	deputation	facilities	juvenile
petition	recreational	responsibility	submission 归顺	subsidise	vexation	vicinity

1 Complete this petition:

As students at the local secondary school, we are annoyed at _____ in the local newspapers about so-

called _____ behaviour among teenagers in the area. We feel it is exaggerated and unfair; more importantly,

we believe it is the council's _____ to provide more _____ _____ in the area

for our age group. We would be most happy to work hard to raise funds if you could give us _____ that you

would _____ such a project.

2 Using appropriate forms of words in the word list, complete these sentences:

a The students _____ that the best site for the centre would be the reserve _____ to the
school.

b The alternative site, in the _____ of the creek, would have flooded occasionally.

c It is easy enough to gain _____ from the council of the need for a _____ centre, but far
more difficult to force action.

d The _____ of funds to several projects must be difficult, as there are so many claimants.

e _____ at continual delays would be excusable.

f _____ is often levelled at people involved in _____ for action on certain issues.

g Some adults won't listen when teenagers try to _____ their opinions.

h It is _____ clear that boredom often leads to _____.

3 Find synonyms from the word list for:

a affirm _____

b apportion _____

c irritated _____

d achieve _____

e censure _____

f plentiful _____

g neighbouring _____

h immature _____

4 Provide the noun forms of the following verbs:

a subsidise _____

b accomplish _____

c assert _____

d criticise _____

e facilitate _____

f submit _____

5 Write the council's reply to the students' petition (see Exercise 1).

Spelling
Unit 20
Word charades

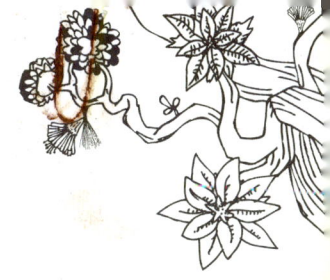

The suffix 'crat' means a member or supporter of a particular government or rule.

alternate	alternative	aristocrat	autocrat	bureaucrat	catalogue	cataract
catastrophe	category	dedication	democrat	desiccation	dogged	dogmatic
incinerating	insinuating	sanction	sanctuary	vulnerable		

1 Find words in the word list ending in 'crat' to match these definitions:

a an official _____

c supporter of democracy _____

b absolute ruler _____

d a person who belongs to a class of nobles _____

2 Highlight the word used incorrectly in the following sentences and find the correct word from the word list:

a When the general attacked, he planned to hit the enemy at its most venerable point. _____

b At the bird sanction, feeding takes place at four o'clock. _____

c Our next door neighbour smokes us out of the house every Sunday when he is insinuating his rubbish. _____

d As the teacher worked long hours the students admired his desiccation to duty. _____

e As the road was boggy and gouged out by the streams, the driver took the alternate route. _____

3 Find words in the word list beginning with 'cat' to match these definitions:

a a complete list _____

c a waterfall _____

b the denouement of a drama _____

d one of a set of classes _____

4 Find words in the word list beginning with 'dog' to match these definitions:

a laying down the law _____

b obstinate _____

5 Draw coloured lines to match these words:

a insinuating   Sundays

b sanction   coconut

c venerable   statement

d alternate   clergyman

e desiccated   conduct

6 Use a form of the words in italics in the blank spaces provided:

a *dedication*: _____ doctor

b *autocrat*: _____ ruler

c *vulnerable*: obvious _____

d *bureaucrat*: _____ government department

7 Make a list of as many words as you can find with the 'crat' ending, including their meanings. Have a class discussion about the meanings of the words.

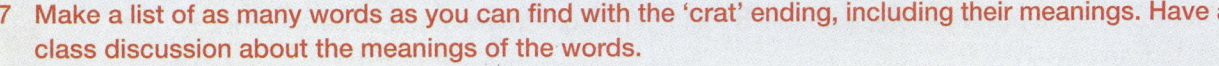

Spelling
Unit 21
Marriage

acquaintance	anecdote	announcement	apologetic	bridal	column	congratulations
detract	difference	documents	engagement	hilarity	introduction	preparations
prospective	solemnity	spouse	reception	torrential		

1 **Explain the differences between:**

a an anecdote and a story: _____

_____

b a spouse and a husband: _____

_____

c cloth and clothe: _____

_____

d hilarity and enjoyment: _____

_____

e an acquaintance and a friend: _____

_____

f a witness and a spectator: _____

_____

g prospective and perspective: _____

_____

2 **Arrange these words that describe rainfall in order of intensity, from least to most:** *drizzling, torrential, soaking, spitting.*

_____

3 **Draw coloured lines to match these sentence halves:**

a An acquaintance introduced me to	in the social column of the local newspaper.
b Torrential rain did not	when anecdotes were told at the reception.
c The announcement of our engagement appeared	were frantic.
d There was much hilarity	my prospective spouse.
e Preparations for the wedding	in the grounds of the Botanic Gardens.
f Dressing the bridal	detract from the solemnity of the occasion.
g Documents, like the marriage licence,	party was expensive.
h The reception was held	were signed in front of witnesses.

4 **Using words from the word list, write an email to a friend describing a wedding ceremony that went wrong (for example, a power failure, a double booking, the non-arrival of the bride/groom, a scuffle between families).**

Spelling
Unit 22
To keep you thinking

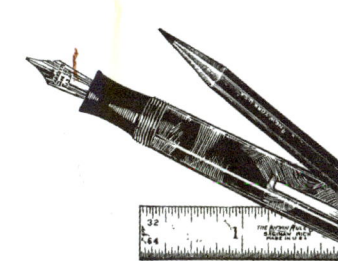

anonymous	arrogant	caricature	chronological	cliché	compassionate	compulsory
contemporary	hierarchy	impassive	impracticable	inaudible	irresolute	loquacious
presentiment	pretentious	rehearsal	rehearse	symmetrical	visual	voluntary

1 Find the words in the word list with these meanings:

a full of pity for _____

b unable to feel emotion _____

c vacillating, lacking determination _____

d forced _____

e a rank order _____

f of one's own free will _____

g unable to be easily carried out _____

h concerned with sight _____

i unable to be heard _____

j living at the same time _____

k talkative _____

l of unknown authorship _____

m haughty and pompous _____

n over-used and hackneyed expression _____

o arranged according to the order of time _____

p balanced, of fine proportions _____

q a premonition, an unfounded expectation _____

q to repeat in order to perfect a performance _____

s an exaggerated and distorted picture of a person _____

t ostentatious _____

2 Choose a suitable word from the word list to use with each of the following:

a concert _____

b phone call _____

c tyrant _____

d speech _____

e plan _____

f order _____

g grim _____

h worker _____

i jarring _____

j fashion _____

k aid _____

l student _____

m headmaster _____

n government _____

o claim _____

p education _____

q benefactor _____

r perfect _____

s cruel _____

t obvious _____

3 Write a caricature of one of the following types of people:

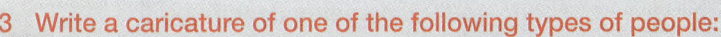

- a nagging wife
- a sulky teenager
- an ignorant buffoon
- a cranky old man.

Spelling
Unit 23
Who is?

autocrat	bailiff	benefactor	botanist	cartographer	counsellor
creditor	curator	debtor	delegate	diplomat	entrepreneur
heroine	hypnotist	interior decorator	legatee	maestro	ombudsman
pathologist	philatelist	physicist	physiologist	veterinarian	

1 Who is described in the following definitions? Choose your answer from the word list:

a a person who analyses blood samples _____

b a custodian of a museum _____

c a person who gives advice _____

d a person who draws maps _____

e a person who decorates interiors of homes and offices _____

f an expert in physics _____

g the main female character in a novel _____

h a person who treats animal diseases _____

i a person to whom you owe money _____

j a person who owes you money _____

k an officer who issues summonses _____

l a person who donates to a cause _____

m a person to whom a legacy is left _____

n a person who undertakes a business or enterprise _____

o a person who governs absolutely _____

p a stamp collector _____

q an official appointed to investigate individuals' complaints against public authorities _____

r a scientist concerned with plants _____

s a distinguished musical conductor _____

t a person who can induce a trance-like state _____

u a person chosen to represent an organisation at a conference _____

2 Form adjectives from:

a pathologist _____   d physicist _____

b heroine _____   e botanist _____

c diplomat _____

3 Research one of the jobs from the word list and deliver a speech to your classmates describing the requirements and personal characteristics necessary.

Spelling
Unit 24
I wish to apply

advertised	advisable	application	available	completed	convenient	delegate
distinction	efficiency	employee	employer	enclosed	experience	interview
initiative	meticulous	photocopy	punctual	receptionist	recommendation	reference
schedule	secretarial					

1 Complete this letter:

I would like to apply for the position of _____ that was _____ in the *Daily Mail* on Saturday,
5 February.

I _____ my VCE in 2006 and enclose a _____ of my final report. Since then I have achieved

distinctions in all subjects in the _____ _____ course conducted by the Bigtown Business Academy. Reports from

that college are _____.

For the past two years I have worked in the office of J. B. Smythe Jones and Co. Importers and Exporters during holidays

so I have some _____ in office routine. I include their reference.

I would be available for an _____ any time after 2:00 p.m. any day of the week, if this is _____
for you.

Thanking you,

Yours faithfully,

Mary M. Noteworthy

2 Find appropriate forms of words in the word list to complete these sentences:

a _____ in newspapers for e _____ t may require an _____ by telephone or by letter.

b It is _____ to type such a letter to show your _____

c It is wise to send a _____ of your _____, enabling you to retain the original.

d Remember, business executives have busy _____, so be _____

e Efficient employers _____ as many tasks as possible to their _____

f Be sure to be immaculately dressed and _____ groomed.

3 You can *delegate* responsibility to others. Use *delegate* in a sentence as a noun. _____

_____

_____

4 Make the following words into their opposites by adding prefixes:

a _____ distinct

b _____ experienced

c _____ complete

d _____ available

e _____ convenient

f _____ advisable

5 Write a letter applying for a job at your local health food store.

Spelling
Unit 25
Tools of the trade

The suffixes 'ic' and 'ical' are often used to form adjectives: the noun *photograph*, for example, becomes the adjective *photographic*.

artistry	astronomer	barometric	chiselled	computer	geologist	gymnasium
machinist	meteorologist	microscope	organisms	photographic	programmer	scalpel
scientific	scissors	surgical	telescopic	thermal	thermometer	

1 Change the following nouns to adjectives:

a economy _____ **c** surgeon _____ **e** botany _____

b geology _____ **d** artist _____ **f** optician _____

2 Draw coloured lines to match the instruments with the people who use them:

a artist	scissors
b doctor	chisel
c surveyor	thermometer
d astronomer	scalpel
e scientist	enlarger
f potter	theodolite
g nurse	trowel
h surgeon	microscope
i photographer	wheel
j bricklayer	stethoscope
k meteorologist	lenses
l geologist	computer
m optician	lathe
n programmer	drill
o wood machinist	barometer
p oil miner	Geiger counter
q gymnast	palette
r sculptor	trapeze
s dressmaker	telescope

3 Expand these word groups into sentences:

a chiselled features _____

b barometric pressure _____

c astronomical proportions _____

d photographic memory _____

e thermal springs _____

4 Write a job description for an actuary or a clown at a children's party. Include their tools of trade.

Spelling
Unit 26
Painting by gorilla wins first prize!

appreciate	collection	connoisseur	emulate	exhibition	gallery	imitate
initial	inspiration	intense	landscape	monotonous	objective	picturesque
portrait	sculptor	subdue	subjective	subscription	statuary	technique
vague	visual	vogue				

1 a Art appreciation is very *subjective*. Does this mean *controversial*, *personal*, *functional* or *artistic*? _____

   b What is the opposite of *subjective*? _____

2 Find a word in the word list meaning:

   a a painting of a person _____

   b a painting of a rural scene _____

   c an expert judge in matters of taste _____

   d a place where paintings are exhibited _____

3 Complete the following, using the appropriate forms of words from the word list:

   a The sea has provided _____ for many painters.

   b The collecting of primitive art is in _____ these days.

   c _____ colours are very restful, while _____ colours reflect vitality and passion.

   d Paintings are appreciated by the _____ senses, while food affects the senses of smell and taste.

   e _____, many painters struggle to obtain recognition.

4 a Art Deco is currently *in vogue*. Does this mean *vague*, *inconsistent*, *in fashion* or *in isolation*? _____

   b Use the words *in vogue* in a sentence: _____

_____

5 Find the appropriate forms of words from the word list that are opposite in meaning to:

   a intense _____   **d** exciting _____

   b ugly _____   **e** objective _____

   c final _____

6 Form verbs from the following words:

   a intense _____

   b collective _____

   c visual _____

   d appreciative _____

7 Using a thesaurus, find six synonyms for the word *imitate*. Use each one in a sentence which shows its meaning.

ambiguous	amphibious	antecedent	antiseptic	detracted	distracted	eligible
exhausted	exhorted	illegible	luxuriant	luxurious	monogamous	monotonous
personal	personnel	precedent	president	receptacle	recipient	superficial
superfluous						

1 Highlight the word used incorrectly in the following sentences and find the correct word from the word list:

a This sentence is amphibious as I can see two meanings to it. _____

b The precedent established a committee to promote cancer research. _____

c When the child grazed her knee, her mother daubed it with antecedent cream. _____

d My sister is delighted as she is dating an illegible young man. _____

e The headmaster explained that teachers were invited to attend two meetings each week and he strongly exhausted

them to do so. _____

f On my retirement I was the receptacle of a gold watch presented to me by the firm. _____

g While it is possible for citizens of some countries to have several wives, monotonous marriage is practised in Western

countries. _____

h By presenting untrue facts to the audience the speaker who followed me distracted from my argument. _____

i The furnishings in the medieval castle were luxuriant. _____

j The damage done to the car in the accident was superfluous _____

2 Draw coloured lines to match these words:

a amphibious   writing

b monotonous   mountaineer

c luxuriant   growth

d superfluous   hair

e exhausted   frog

f illegible   repetition

3 Use *personal* and *personnel* in sentences to show their meanings: _____

_____

_____

4 Use a form of the words in italics in the blank spaces provided:

a *personal*: bright _____   **d** *exhausted*: _____ enquiry

b *eligible*: _____ for the position   **e** *monotonous*: irritating _____

c *luxurious*: a life of _____   **f** *distracted*: annoying _____

**5 Research the prefix 'anti'. What does it mean? Find as many words as possible which use the prefix
'anti' and give their meanings.**

Spelling
Unit 28
Wordwise

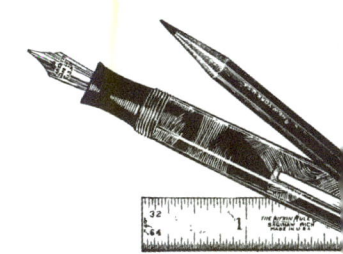

disseminate	dissociate	eject	electrification	electrocution	fluent	fluid
genocide	germicide	indispensable	indisputable	judicial	judicious	official
officious	reject	stereophonic	stereotype	veracious	voracious	

1 Highlight the word used incorrectly in the following sentences and find the correct word from the word list:

a The veracious lion rapidly devoured its catch. _____

b The electrocution of the state railways would speed up travel over the long distances. _____

c I disapprove of the Court's verdict. Sentencing the man to death is judicious murder. _____

d Because of my long association with the firm, I believed I had become indisputable. _____

e I wish to disseminate myself from this group of radicals whose views are contrary to mine. _____

f A powerful genocide is needed to clean the surgeon's hands before he operates. _____

g The fighter pilot, realising that her plane was going to explode, decided to reject herself. _____

h The headmaster told the student that the complaint against him was justified and would be made officious.

_____

i When violent demonstrations were expected at the meeting, John was elected to speak because he was fluid in French.

_____

2 Draw coloured lines to match these words:

a veracious   ideas

b judicious   argument

c officious   fences

d fluid   account

e indisputable   movement

f disseminate   counsellor

g electric   interrogator

3 Complete these sentence fragments:

a Rejecting the decision of the Arbitration Court, _____

b The dissemination of seditious material _____

c Fear of being electrocuted _____

d Overseas, Australians are stereotyped as _____

4 Find words in the word list (or forms of them) to use in the spaces below:

a _____ soap   **d** spoke _____

b _____ appetite   **e** _____ himself from

c _____ the proposal   **f** _____ shock

5 Explain the difference between *veracious* and *voracious*, using an illustration or photo.

Spelling
Unit 29
Bargains galore!

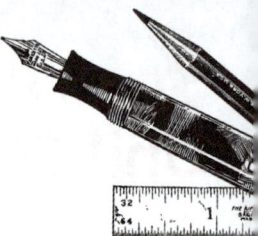

affirmation	ascension	callous	comical	demotion	deplete	epilogue
ferocity	integrity	morose	negation	opaque	privation	prologue
replenishment	segregation	sensitivity	sufficiency	superiority	transparency	

1 Draw coloured lines to match the words from Column 1 with their antonyms in Column 2:

Column 1	Column 2
malevolent	integrate
transparent	injurious
attractive	morose
serious	benevolent
beneficial	opaque
inconspicuous	radical
cheerful	deplete
conservative	repulsive
replenish	noticeable
segregate	comical

Column 1	Column 2
affirm	gentleness
promote	descent
prologue	inferiority
privation	indolently
ferocity	negate
superiority	demote
ascent	sufficiency
sensitively	conscientiously
energetically	callously
irresponsibly	epilogue

2 Use a form of the words in italics in the spaces provided:

a *malevolent*: undisguised _____

b *transparent*: photographic _____

c *sensitive*: obvious _____

d *indolent*: blatant _____

e *integrated*: _____ of races

f *irresponsible*: _____ of the vandals

g *segregated*: _____ of the sexes

h *replenished*: _____ of supplies

i *affirmed*: instant _____

j *promote*: rapid _____

k *noticeable*: _____ moved

l *deprivation*: _____ circumstances

3 Complete these sentence fragments:

a Inconspicuous in the dark _____

b Dressed conservatively _____

c Following his demotion _____

d Deprived of the advantage she thought she had _____

4 Write a letter to a student newspaper, giving your opinion on one of the following topics:

* Promotion by seniority or ability?

* Financial aid for developing countries

* This generation is callous in its treatment of the aged

* Indolence is a modern disease

Spelling
Unit 30
Heroes and villains

contemptible	contemptuous	devious	disrespect	enmity	forbidding	frustration
impertinent	impolite	insidious	irritability	gaunt	lurch	resentment
revulsion	shuffle	slouch	supercilious	swagger	unprincipled	

1. Choose an unpleasant character from a film or television show and describe them, using some of the following words to give a larger-than-life portrait. Add some descriptive words of your own as well.

Appearance: dishevelled, threatening, huge, bedraggled, unkempt, grovelling

Tone of voice: obsequious, smarmy, rude, ingratiating, slimy, impolite, scornful, sneering

Movement: slouch, mince, shuffle, lurch, waddle, swagger

Facial expression: pinched, contemptuous, gaunt, unsmiling, forbidding, frowning

Character: insidious, villainous, contemptible, snobbish, devious

Attitude: supercilious, contemptuous, impertinent, unprincipled, slippery

2. Find and list words that could be used to describe a hero: _____
_____
_____

3. Use a form of the words in italics in the spaces provided:

   a *habit*: _____ action

   b *frustration*: _____ task

   c *impertinent*: unwarranted _____

   d *scornful*: filled with _____

   e *forbidding*: _____ fruit

   f *disrespect*: _____ glance

   g *snobbish:* foolish _____

4. Find antonyms for the following words:

   a forbidding _____

   b enmity _____

   c devious _____

   d contemptuous _____

   e irritable _____

   f revulsion _____

5. Give four synonyms for *villain*: _____
_____

6. A *caricature* is a representation (usually comic) of a person, exaggerating their traits. Find a cartoon in the newspaper that caricatures someone in the news and explain how the caricature works to ridicule its subject.

Spelling

Spelling
Unit 31
The uranium debate

alternative	conservation	considerations	controversy	depletion	disposal	environment
exposure	formulate	mutation	nuclear	policies	politicians	potential
precautions	proliferation	propaganda	radiation	rational	reactors	subsequent
terrorist	uranium	vehemently				

1 The mining of uranium has long been a controversial issue. Using words from the word list, complete the following major considerations:

a Despite programs for the _____ of energy, existing resources are being rapidly _____

b Protection of the _____

c Siting of _____ power stations.

d _____ of waste from nuclear reactors.

e _____ sources of energy such as solar power.

f The increased prospect of _____ warfare.

g Increased exposure to _____

2 Complete this table:

Verb	Adjective	Noun
terrorise	terrorist	terrorism
		radiation
consider		
	exposed	
ration		

3 Complete these sentence fragments:

a Radioactive dust _____

b The proliferation of ideas _____

c Subsequently, solar energy _____

4 Draw coloured lines to match these words:

a propaganda   alteration

b deplete   safeguard

c vehement   spreading

d proliferation   reduce

e mutation   intense

f precaution   publicity

5 Write a letter to the Prime Minister giving your opinion on the use of nuclear power. Try to use some of the words from the word list.

Spelling
Unit 32
Bargain book sale

agitator	anxious	assaulted	barriers	dislodge	effected	encounter
escalator	extricate	fertiliser	flexed	grievously	guise	ignominiously
inflicted	infuriated	intention	laughter	obstacle	outmanoeuvred	panic
precariously	reinforcements	retreat	scheme	stalwart	strategic	undeterred

1   Fill in the blanks using words from the word list:

Sale time was here again. Like a racehorse in the Melbourne Cup, I _____ my muscles outside the doors of the

bookshop waiting for the b _____ rs to fall. At last they did and, racing for position, I was caught with two

s _____ t competitors between the door rails. Und _____ d by the crowd, I managed to

e _____ e myself and outstripped my inf _____ d and a _____ s rivals. My

_____ was to avoid a similar en _____ r on the _____, by using the stairs.

Arriving at the second floor, which was overcrowded with confused and somewhat panicky shoppers vainly searching for

limited stock, I faced the _____ course. Dodging, leaping, sliding, creeping, crawling, weeping, I reached a pile

of books balancing p _____ y on top of a tall stepladder.

There it was: *The Poetry of John Donne* ig _____ y squeezed between *A Handbook for Agitators* and *Wee*

Willie Winkie. I managed to dis _____ it, but, in so doing, I was gr _____ y as _____ d

by *The Napoleonic Wars* and out _____ d by *Garden Fertilisers*, which _____ a savage blow on

my forehead. As re _____ ts in the g _____ e of *Ballet Dancing* in six volumes were on the way,

I escaped, paid for the book and e _____ d a str _____ c withdrawal from the shop.

2   Find synonyms from the word list for:

a withdrawal _____

b disentangle _____

c enraged _____

d hindrance _____

e sturdy _____

f meeting _____

g determined _____

3   What is the past tense of *panic*? _____

4   What words or forms of word from the list mean:

a feeling of injured innocence _____

d sturdy _____

b perilous or uncertain _____

e worried _____

c humiliating _____

f pretence _____

5   Write an email to a friend about a bargain that turned out to be a disaster.

Spelling
Unit 33
Confounding words

accompaniment	acknowledge	acquaintance	apologetic	argument	character
conscience	contemporary	correspondence	definite	disintegrate	environment
honourable	humorous	interpretation	intellectual	intervention	liaison
naïve	occurred	optimistic	perseverance	prejudiced	privilege
psychology	questionnaire	rhythm	scene	skilful	soliloquy
surveillance	tragedy				

1 Find words from the word list that mean:

a take notice of _____

b study of mental processes _____

c shatter, break up _____

d innocent _____

e part of an act in a play _____

f dexterous _____

g quarrel _____

h happened _____

i opposite to pessimistic _____

j biased _____

k sad event; calamity _____

l beat _____

m special favour _____

n comic _____

o watch _____

p supporting act _____

q worthy of praise, esteem _____

r agreement _____

s subjective explanation _____

t regretful _____

u moral sense of right and wrong _____

v mental or moral qualities _____

w enlightened or learned person _____

x belonging to the same time _____

y a person known slightly _____

z connection or co-operation between two parties _____

aa steadfast pursuit of an aim _____

2 Use the appropriate forms of words from the word list to complete the following:

a _____ on viewing habits

b a _____ answer

c _____ beat of the tomtoms

d _____ student

e _____ by satellite

f _____ classes in society

g _____ in the argument

h _____ the receipt of

i _____ moment

j the meteor _____ on impact

k _____ anecdote

l _____ nature

m _____ with our solicitor

n _____ tone of voice

o _____ between the two groups

p _____ literature

q _____ with the problem

r _____ with the difficult task

s _____ wrought

t Macbeth's _____

3 Hold a spelling competition in class, using the words from the word list.

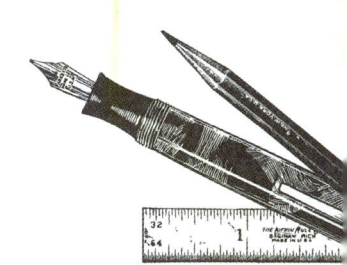

Spelling
Unit 34
Twenty questions 2

Choose a word circle. Working in pairs, make up a list of twenty questions based on the activities used in these units, for example:

a   Spell the word _____

b   Give a synonym/antonym for _____

c   Form a descriptive word from _____

Use your questions to test the rest of your class.

interruption
constitution
resolution   contribution
substitution   allocation
recreation   deprivation
deputation   accommodation
prohibition   intervention
rejection   justification
recognition   definition
interpretation

transference
prevalence   malevolence   benevolence
inference   reference   impudence   occurrence   resilience
emergence   persistence   diligence   independence   insolence
competence   eloquence   evidence   indolence
indulgence   prevalence   presence
difference   permanence

prosecute   persecute   veracity
voracity   judicious   judicial   allusion   illusion   infer
imply   compliment   complement   formally   formerly   prospective
perspective   rhyme   rhythm   sedentary   sedimentary
individual   person   character   personality

incomprehensible
negligible
responsible   contemptible
convertible   discernible
invisible   indelible   inedible
inexhaustible   irresistible
invincible   susceptible
permissible   irrepressible
accessible   compatible
fallible   plausible
feasible

profusion
fusion   delusion   seclusion
illusion   allusion   persuasion
dissuasion   abrasion   confusion
derision   adhesion
precision

impetuous
strenuous   arduous
tenuous   inconspicuous
innocuous   virtuous
continuous   judicious
ostentatious   pretentious
conscientious   contagious
vicious   precocious
suspicious   unconscious
spacious   malicious

convenient
competent
dependent   resilient
permanent   indulgent
insolent   indolent   persistent
different   deficient   diligent
confident   impudent
fluent   equivalent   evident
eloquent   emergent
insurgent   apparent
obedient

Amanda Ford
Elizabeth Haywood

Part 3
Comprehension

This section is designed to help students consolidate comprehension skills in the context of enjoyable, contemporary and classic material. Within 17 double-page units, a wide range of material is presented, including extracts from novels and magazines, poems, newspaper articles and instructional material. The emphasis is on providing different styles and genres of writing in order to lead students towards a detailed understanding of written material. Questions are grouped into:

- What is being said? (literal comprehension)
- What does it mean? (inferential or interpretive comprehension)
- What do I think about it? (evaluative or implied comprehension)

Students' responses will consist of both short answers and more sustained pieces of writing, with the opportunity for extension work provided for in the 'What do I think about it?' section. Questions should generally be answered in complete sentences and any writing to be completed off the page is indicated by the icon.

The mobile phone has been a part of our lives since the 1980s. It enables us to stay in contact with our family and friends at all times and in most areas. However, because of the quick acceptance and proliferation of mobiles into our lives, we have missed out on an important step, namely, the etiquette of their use. Here is a description of 'proper' phone usage in many common situations.

DRIVING A CAR

Do not use your phone while you are driving! You could be distracted by the gossip you are hearing and forget to look where you are going, or you could take your eyes off the road to look at the phone's display or to press in a number. Either way, you could cause a nasty accident.

IN A RESTAURANT

There is probably nothing more irritating than a restaurant patron receiving or making a call near you when you are in a restaurant. The icy glares you receive should be warning enough that it is not appreciated. Turn your phone off and use your message service to return calls after you leave.

AT THE CINEMA

Do not succumb to the urge to call a friend if the film is boring, or if you want to find out what happens. You could cause a riot—with you as the target of all the enraged cinema customers.

IN THE CLASSROOM

Using your phone in the classroom is very bad manners. It is an insult to the teacher who probably has a packed curriculum to impart in a relatively short time.

AT THE THEATRE

There is no more icy glare than that of a theatre patron who has paid a lot of money to see a show and hears your phone playing a cute tune. It goes without saying that you will be seen as a social pariah in this situation.

ATTENDING A LECTURE

Your lecturer will not appreciate hearing your conversation. Once again, switch off—do not even consider using the SMS service, either, as that is also very distracting.

IN HOSPITALS

This is probably the most important place to make sure your phone is switched off. Your phone can interfere with life-saving electronic equipment in hospitals, so it is imperative that your phone is switched off before you enter.

ON PLANES

Your phone might interfere with navigational equipment and cause a dreadful accident so you should switch it off before boarding a plane.

As you can see, mobile phone etiquette is quite complicated. However, it is worth it to show some courtesy to those around us, and hold our private conversations in suitable locations.

What is being said?

1 Definitions: what is the meaning of the following?

a etiquette _____

b proliferation _____

c patron _____

d succumb _____

e enraged _____

f curriculum _____

g impart _____

h social pariah _____

 i SMS _____

 j imperative _____

 k navigational equipment _____

2 What important aspect of the use of mobile phones has been neglected? _____

3 How could you cause an accident by using your mobile in a car (two ways)? _____

_____

_____

4 What should warn you not to use your mobile in a restaurant? _____

_____

5 How could you cause a riot in the cinema? _____

_____

6 Why should you not use your phone in the classroom? _____

_____

7 Why would you be seen as a social outcast at the theatre? _____

_____

8 What is the problem with using your SMS in a lecture? _____

_____

9 How could your mobile be deadly in a hospital? _____

_____

10 What problems can a mobile cause on a plane? _____

_____

What does it mean?

11 Why is mobile phone etiquette needed? _____

_____

_____

_____

12 Sometimes it can be annoying to others when you use your mobile. At other times it can actually be dangerous. Draw up two columns and list occasions when it could be either annoying or dangerous.

What do I think about it?

13 How has the mobile phone changed people's behaviour?

14 Write a pleading note to your parent or guardian outlining your reasons for wanting the latest mobile phone. Then write the reply.

Comprehension
Unit 2
Owe, owe, owe. Oh no!

Susie O'Brien
Herald Sun

Bankers act like Santa by offering all sorts of credit card goodies but—beware—they are luring customers into depressing days of debt.

In your house is Christmas cheer giving way to credit card catastrophe?

Has all that loving and giving been replaced with a sinking feeling in the pit of your stomach about how you're going to pay for it all?

You're not alone.

The sad truth is that many banks and lenders don't ever want you to pay off your credit card bill in full.

Research shows they are using increasingly sophisticated techniques to trap us into borrowing more than we can pay off in full every month.

So you owe, you owe, it's off to work you go.

The first trick is the little box at the top of your bill that says 'minimum payment'.

According to a study by British psychologist Neil Stewart released this month, the minimum payment amounts on credit card bills lead people to pay on average 43 per cent less off per month than they would otherwise do.

When the banks give us permission to pay off less than we can afford, we usually accept the invitation—who wouldn't?

As *The Economist* notes, this means many of us end up paying roughly twice the amount of interest—usually hundreds and hundreds of our hard-earned dollars.

Just paying off the minimum allowable —usually 5 per cent of the total bill—means you end up paying

almost a third more than you've originally borrowed.

Consumer Affairs Victoria modelling shows that if you have a $2000 balance payable at 18.5 per cent, and you only pay the minimum, and don't borrow any more, you'll take seven years and end up paying an extra $820 in interest.

So your little preppie will be in high school before you've cleared this year's Christmas debt.

But CAV studies also show most people don't understand how interest rates work, or how interest-free periods are calculated.

And banks are, well, banking on it.

Welcome to trick number two.

Rather than clarify things, their ads tell us credit cards promote savings and you can live well despite being in debt.

A CAV study released this year found we want to believe what banks tell us because it lets us keep on spending and we can worry about it later. Wrong.

This brings us to trick number three.

One of the best ways banks and other lenders use to trap us is to issue unsolicited invitations for us to boost out credit limits—often by as much as $3000.

People accept because they want the money and because they trust that if banks are offering it to them, then they can afford to accept it. Wrong again.

The same CAV survey found consumers received more direct approaches to boost their credit limit just before and just after Christmas.

They found that limit increase offers were aimed at those who were unable

to pay their monthly balance in full or who had recently made large purchases.

It's all so wrong.

Why are they allowed to prey on us when we are vulnerable, and monitor our accounts, waiting for the right time to pounce?

Why are they inducing us to go further into debt without testing whether we have the means to pay it all back?

The lack of regulation is truly astonishing.

But so is the acceptance of many people. What about just spending less and living within your means? Just because you can buy things on credit doesn't mean you can afford them.

Just because it's on sale doesn't mean it's a bargain if you're buying it on credit and racking up huge interest bills.

Now, I know how hard it is to resist what looks like a bargain when you've got a credit card burning a hole in your pocket.

I also know first-hand how keen lenders are to get us into debt.

To our amazement, my husband and I recently were given an extra $20 000 credit on two cards after buying a couch interest free, and refinancing our home loan.

But ultimately, our spending is our responsibility, and no one is holding a gun to your head making us buy that Nintendo Wii or 46in plasma TV.

However, lenders and banks should also be held accountable for trying to keep our credit card accounts in the red indefinitely.

What is being said?

1 Definitions: what is the meaning of the following?

a   vulnerable _____

b   inducement _____

    c   refinance _____

    d   accountable _____

2 Why are bankers compared to Santa? _____

_____

3 What, according to the writer, is the 'sad truth'? _____

_____

4 'You owe, you owe, it's off to work you go.' What cartoon movie does this refer to? _____

_____

5 List the three tricks used by banks to make the customer pay more. _____

_____

_____

_____

6 If you pay off only the minimum allowable on your credit card, how much more than you borrowed could you end up paying?

_____

7 Why do we want to believe what banks tell us, according to a CAV study? _____

_____

8 Which two groups of people are most likely to be invited to increase their credit limit? _____

_____

9 The writer concludes with two seemingly contradictory points in the last two sentences. What are they?

_____

_____

What does it mean?

10 Explain the pun in the heading. _____

_____

Comprehension

11 The writer uses a number of rhetorical questions in her article. (A rhetorical question is used for emphasis and requires no answer. The answer is implied in the actual question.) When she asks 'Why are they allowed to prey on us when we are vulnerable...?' she is attempting to make the reader think about the problem and the need for more regulation of the banks. Find another rhetorical question in the article and suggest the reason the writer might have used it.

What do I think about it?

12 Write an email to a friend, suggesting ways you can both avoid a large credit card debt when you go on holiday or buy an expensive item.

Comprehension
Unit 3
Only the traffic is a cross to bear

Alan Hill
Herald Sun

The wide, tree-lined avenue in downtown Hanoi is a fast-flowing stream of bicycles and motor-bikes.

Step off the footpath slowly but confidently, advises a local, cross the road at a leisurely pace and do not stop.

Without slowing, the bike riders diverge slightly to the right or the left, calculating our rate of progress and missing us by centimetres.

Confidence is the key for the traveller in Vietnam. The traffic will not mow you down, the locals are friendly, the countryside is beautiful and the food is flavoursome and healthy.

Hanoi, the capital and cultural centre of Vietnam, is a stylish and gracious city that retains its old-world charm.

Visitors are often surprised to find that its French colonial heritage survived the American War, as the Vietnam War is called locally.

Much of central Hanoi is best explored by walking, particularly the Old Quarter, where narrow streets are lined with colourful shop-houses selling herbal medicines, bright fabrics, silver and jade jewellery.

A trip to Hanoi would be incomplete without visiting the father of modern Vietnam, Ho Chi Minh, whose embalmed body is on display in a huge marble mausoleum at Ba Dinh Square.

A thousand kilometres to the south is bright and brassy Ho Chi Minh City, which most people still call Saigon. Everywhere you look there is colour and movement. Below silvery skyscrapers, schoolgirls in their traditional long white tunics chat on mobile phones. Modern shopping centres are just streets away from long-established markets and ancient pagodas.

In Cholon, Ho Chi Minh City's bustling Chinatown district, the huge, covered Binh Tay market is packed solid with merchandise.

The ground floor is devoted to food of all kinds, including tiny rose apples, lotus seeds, camomile for making tea, orange fruit used for dyeing rice, century-old eggs covered in rice husk or charcoal paste.

From the city's landmark Notre Dame Cathedral, built by the French in the 1880s, a stroll along Dong Khoi street takes you past many new boutiques and galleries as well as some of the city's best restaurants and bars.

Reunification Hall is the former Presidential Palace, home to the past three presidents. This is where tanks crashed through the gates in April 1975, an event which came to symbolise the end of the Vietnam War.

What is being said?

1 Definitions: what is the meaning of the following?

a cross to bear _____

b leisurely _____

c diverge _____

d old-world charm _____

e French colonial heritage _____

f embalmed _____

g mausoleum _____

h lotus _____

i brassy _____

j pagodas _____

k symbolise _____

2 What are the main forms of transport in downtown Hanoi? _____

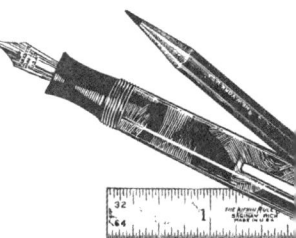

3 What is the advice of a local about crossing the road? _____

_____

4 How is Hanoi described in the fifth paragraph? _____

_____

5 What often surprises visitors to Hanoi? _____

_____

6 What, according to this article, would complete your visit to Hanoi? _____

_____

7 Where is Ho Chi Minh City in relation to Hanoi? _____

8 What was the old name for Ho Chi Minh City? _____

9 Ho Chi Minh City is a mixture of ancient and modern. Give two examples of this mixture. _____

_____

_____

10 What five foods could you find at Binh Tay Market? _____

_____

11 What is a landmark of Ho Chi Minh City? _____

12 What happened at the former Presidential Palace in April 1975? _____

_____

What does it mean?

13 Why is the traffic the only 'cross to bear' in Hanoi, according to this article? _____

_____

_____

14 Why is walking the best way to explore the Old Quarter? _____

_____

_____

15 Compare Hanoi with Ho Chi Minh City, using information from this article. How are they different? _____

_____

_____

What do I think about it?

16 Which of the two cities described appeals to you the most? Give reasons for your answer.

17 Write a travel article about a place you have visited (it could be close to home). Try to describe its appeal and the amenities available. What was the food like? (About 150 words.)

Comprehension
Unit 4
Survival of the meanest

Greg Thom

Herald Sun

Just like everyday life, gamers are often asked to make moral choices. Games writer Greg Thom ponders the moral dilemmas triggered by video games

FALLOUT 3 (PC/PS3/XBOX 360)

Set in Washington D.C. 200 years after a nuclear holocaust destroyed most of America, *Fallout 3* offers a vast, devastated landscape to explore and tantalising choice of characters to inhabit.

From the start as a newborn baby, players select attributes—strength, agility and intelligence—that shape their character as they grow to adulthood.

Once you leave the safety of your fallout shelter, every action and interaction will affect your karma level and influence how you are perceived.

It may be tempting to steal the unattended food, pick a fellow character's pocket or lie in order to advance, but all will decrease your karma.

Follow a more pious moral compass and you might receive a better reception the next time you meet a pack of armed-to-the-teeth strangers.

GRAND THEFT AUTO IV (PC/PS3/XBOX 360)

Of all the games that give players a clear choice between right and wrong, the GTA series is perhaps the easiest to be tempted to the dark side.

No one forces you to mug the woman crossing the road and steal her cash before carjacking a vehicle and breaking every law in the book fleeing the cops.

The fact that you can do all these terrible things is a huge part of the game's appeal. Follow the mission-based game-play or break free and do what you want. In fact, there are benefits for doing so. Committing crimes and getting away with them increases your notoriety with the police and street cred.

Mind you, it also increases your chances of being caught—a humiliating experience that empties your pockets before you're turned back on to the streets.

BIOSHOCK (PC/PS3/XBOX 360)

After barely surviving a plane crash, you seek sanctuary in Rapture, a failed utopian underwater city that has been torn apart by greed and civil war and its inhabitants' passion for genetic engineering has made them homicidal mutants.

Praised for its dynamic game-play, intelligent characters and art deco attention to detail, *Bioshock* presents players with moral choices at every turn.

Do you exploit the city's innocent inhabitants for your own aims ... or try to save them?

What is being said?

1 Definitions: what is the meaning of the following?

a holocaust _____

b karma _____

c pious _____

d the dark side _____

e notoriety _____

f Utopia _____

g art deco _____

2 What does the heading imply about the games? _____

3 What is the setting for the game *Fallout 3*? _____

4 What is a moral dilemma? _____

_____

5 How can you increase your karma level in *Fallout 3*? _____

_____

6 What is the advantage of increasing your karma? _____

_____

7 Why does the reviewer say that it is easy to be tempted to the dark side when you play *Grand Theft Auto IV*?

_____

_____

8 What is the setting for the game *Bioshock*? _____

9 Describe the inhabitants of Rapture. _____

_____

10 Why has *Bioshock* been praised? _____

_____

What does it mean?

11 To what extent has the writer really 'pondered the moral dilemmas triggered by video games'? _____

_____

_____

_____

_____

12 What sort of gamers might be attracted to each of these games?

_____

_____

_____

_____

_____

_____

What do I think about it?

13 Which of the three games reviewed above would appeal to you the most? Give reasons for your answer.

14 Write a review of one of your favourite games for a teen magazine, including the moral choices the game includes.

Comprehension

We were schooner-rigged and rakish, with a long and lissome hull,
And we flew the pretty colours of the cross-bones and the skull;
We'd a big black Jolly Roger flapping grimly at the fore,
And we sailed the Spanish Water in the happy days of yore.

We'd long brass gun amidships, like a well-conducted ship,
We had each a brace of pistols and a cutlass at the hip;
It's a point which tells against us, and a fact to be deplored,
But we chased the goodly merchant-men and laid their ships aboard.

Then the dead men fouled the scuppers and the wounded filled the chains,
And the paint-work all was spatter-dashed with other people's brains,
She was boarded, she was looted, she was scuttled till she sank.
And the pale survivors left us by the medium of the plank.

O! then it was (while standing by the taffrail on the poop)
We could hear the drowning folk lament the absent chicken-coop;
Then, having washed the blood away, we'd little else to do
Than to dance a quiet hornpipe as the old salts taught us to.

O! the fiddle on the fo'c'sle, and the slapping naked soles,
And the genial 'Down the middle, Jake, and curtsey when she rolls!'
With the silver seas around us and the pale moon overhead,
And the look-out not a-looking and his pipe-bowl glowing red.

Ah! the pig-tailed, quidding pirates and the pretty pranks we played,
All have since been put a stop-to by the naughty Board of Trade;
The schooners and the merry crews are laid away to rest,
A little south the sunset in the Islands of the Blest.

By John Masefield, 1902

What is being said?

1 Definitions: what is the meaning of the following?

a schooner _____

b rakish _____

c lissome _____

d hull _____

e Spanish Water _____

f yore _____

g amidships _____

h brace _____

i fouled _____

j scuppers _____

k scuttled _____

l taffrail _____

m poop _____

n fo'c'sle _____

o quidding _____

2 What does the Jolly Roger look like? _____

3 What weapons did the pirates and their ship carry? _____

_____

4 What did the pirates do to the merchant ships? _____

_____

5 What did the pirates do to the crew of the merchant ships? Support your answer with evidence from the poem.

_____

_____

_____

6 What happened to any survivors? _____

7 What did the pirates do when they had finished their bloodthirsty deeds? _____

_____

What does it mean?

8 What is your impression of these pirates? Give an example from the poem to support your answer.

_____

_____

9 How does the writer of this poem seem to feel about his days as a pirate? _____

_____

_____

10 What do you think he means when he says: 'The schooner and the merry crews are laid away to rest/A little south the sunset in the Islands of the Blest'?

_____

_____

11 Why would the Board of Trade have wanted to stamp out piracy? _____

_____

_____

What do I think about it?

12 Imagine you are a young cabin boy or cabin girl in John Silver's crew. Write another verse about your experiences, using the rhythm of the original ballad as your model.

BEAUTY THERAPIST

Can you take the responsibility of establishing, co-ordinating and promoting a new beauty salon? Are you enthusiastic and dedicated? Do you have previous experience in the industry? If you can answer 'yes' to all of these questions please phone after 9 am Monday to make an appointment for an interview.

CROWD CONTROLLERS

Experienced crowd controllers needed for permanent position in the eastern suburbs. Gaming licence preferred but not essential. Must have own transport and phone. Contact John or send résumé to Box 197.

LABOURER

Labourer required for timber yard in Malvern area. Must be willing to learn about timber industry. Must be of neat appearance and have forklift licence. References essential. Good wages and conditions for the right person. Phone Jill after 9 am Monday.

RESTAURANT SUPERVISOR

To work in a busy complex consisting of two function rooms and a restaurant. Must be motivated, extremely well presented and be a team player. Must be able to lead by example and have sound knowledge of the catering and hospitality industries. Excellent remuneration. This is a full-time position requiring work at weekends and evenings. Written résumés, including names of three referees, to Mary at Box 0432.

TELEMARKETING

Due to an increase in business, Reflex Communications require extra telemarketers. You must be motivated, goal-oriented, a good communicator, willing to work for incentives and bonuses and available to work weekends and evenings. Immediate start and training. Base rate $15 per hour. Phone Cassie to arrange an interview.

What is being said?

1 Definitions: what is the meaning of the following?

a beauty therapist _____

b coordinate _____

c promoting _____

d gaming licence _____

e forklift licence _____

f motivated _____

g catering industry _____

h hospitality industry _____

i remuneration _____

j résumé _____

k referee _____

l goal-oriented _____

m incentives _____

2 What personal qualities are required of the beauty therapist? _____

3 What are the three main responsibilities of the beauty therapist, as outlined in the advertisement? _____

_____

_____

4 When should an applicant for the beauty therapist's job call? _____

5 Is the crowd controller required to have a gaming licence? _____

6 What two documents would the applicant for the labourer's position need to provide? _____

_____

7 List five qualities required for the restaurant supervisor's position. _____

_____

_____

8 How many referees are needed for the restaurant supervisor's position? _____

9 Why are extra telemarketers required? _____

10 List the five requirements of the prospective telemarketer. _____

_____

_____

What does it mean?

11 Why would the crowd controller need a car and a phone? _____

_____

_____

12 Why would the timber yard require the labourer to be 'of neat appearance'? _____

_____

_____

13 How could the restaurant supervisor be both a leader and a team player? _____

_____

_____

_____

14 List the qualities required by the telemarketer in order of importance, as you see them. _____

_____

_____

What do I think about it?

15 Write a letter of application for one of these jobs. Make sure it is one that will accept a written application. Try to sell yourself and your qualities. Refer to the job requirements in your letter. (About 150 words)

Comprehension
Unit 7
The Hidden

In the middle of the night, her shelter was torn away by the shrieking wind. Terrified, and only half functioning, Jess struggled eastwards. Mangroves thrashed, clattered and writhed around her in a dance of destruction. Broken branches and debris were hurled at her. She felt as though she was being beaten by a thousand digging sticks. Was it the spirits of her mother's people?

After what seemed like hours of struggle, she fought clear of the mangroves. Surging water and mud gave way to firm ground. Now more open to the battering wind, she dragged herself into the meagre shelter of a small outcrop of rock.

Although exhausted, sleep was impossible as unbroken rain deluged the land and the earth disappeared beneath a rush of water. She huddled on a mound of rock. Her heart cried. Was this what she had escaped Beattie for? Truly, the spirits must hate her. In her misery, she thought if she could lie down, she would never get up again. Nothing could be worse than this.

But, she was not taken. Life refused to leave her body.

Finally, a hint of daylight diluted the black sky. The rain eased. The girl creaked her joints into motion and staggered away in search of a better shelter. She needed somewhere to lie down, be warm and sleep. Her thin dress was moulded to her skin and the wind on its wet fibres sucked the last of the warmth from her body. Detesting it, a white man thing, she stripped it off. She almost threw it away, but checked. She may have need of it.

Behind her, the belt of mangrove country was a bent and broken jungle of desolation. Tide and wind-driven water stretched hungry fingers of mud deep into the land. Jess staggered towards a bigger outcrop. Previously hidden by the earlier belting rain, it might contain a crevice or tiny cave she could crawl into.

As she approached it she skirted a tidal creek on her right. Her numbed mind recorded the fact. Creeks carried fish. But first, the need for warmth and sleep overrode everything else. Head down, she plodded towards the outcrop.

She jarred to a stop. Stupefied with exhaustion, it took long moments for it to make sense. A body lay at her feet.

From the novel *The Hidden* by Ron Bunney

What is being said?

1 Definitions: what is the meaning of the following?

a writhed _____

b mangroves _____

c debris _____

d surging _____

e meagre _____

f outcrop _____

g deluged _____

h diluted _____

i desolation _____

j crevice _____

k plod _____

l jarred _____

2 What happened to Jess's shelter? _____

3 What did Jess think the storm might represent? _____

4 Where did she shelter? _____

5 Who was she running away from? _____

6 What did she feel she could do in her misery? _____

_____

7 Why did Jess move on at daybreak? _____

8 Why didn't she throw away the dress? _____

9 Why did Jess head for a bigger outcrop of rocks? _____

_____

10 What could be useful about the creek she walked around? _____

11 What were her two main desires? _____

_____

12 What did she see lying at her feet? _____

What does it mean?

13 Why do you think Jess was only 'half functioning' as she struggled eastwards? _____

_____

_____

14 What is the 'dance of destruction'? _____

_____

_____

15 Why was she more open to the wind when she reached firm ground? _____

_____

_____

16 How did Jess feel about the dress she takes off? _____

_____

_____

17 Why is the mud described in terms of fingers? _____

_____

_____

18 What would it be like to feel 'stupefied with exhaustion'? _____

_____

What do I think about it?

19 What happens next? Where has the body come from? How did it get there? What does Jess do next? Continue the story. (About 250 words)

The 2008 Board Election process has commenced. Election material has been mailed to all members with the October edition of RoyalAuto. Where multiple members are at the same address, the first member will receive the election material with RoyalAuto and separate packs have been mailed to each other member eligible to vote.

Ballot packs are also available at RACV Shops.

VOTING INFORMATION

The 2008 Board Election is a postal vote. You cannot vote using this website. For the convenience of members, ballot boxes are located at RACV Shop at 438 Little Collins Street and on the ground floor of the City Club at 501 Bourke Street.

Each Election pack includes information about the Candidates standing for election, ballot paper, ballot envelope and reply paid envelope.

ELIGIBILITY TO VOTE

Each eligible member is allowed only one vote in this ballot regardless of the number of memberships held or the number of vehicles under a single membership.

Members who have joined after 1 March 2008 are not eligible to vote in this election.

View the Candidates (pdf 425KB).

CATEGORIES OF MEMBERSHIP PERMITTED TO VOTE:

Service Members
Ordinary (Club) Members
Personal Members

CATEGORIES OF MEMBERSHIP NOT PERMITTED TO VOTE:

Honorary Members
Temporary Members
Manufacturers' Assistance Program
Absentee Members
Associate Corporate Members
Relationship Members

HOW TO VOTE

Instructions for voting are contained with the Candidate Statements and Voting Instructions.

If you wish to vote, you must only vote for two candidates. Vote by placing a tick in only two boxes on the ballot paper. If you place a tick in fewer than two or more than two boxes your vote will be invalid.

Place the ballot paper in the ballot envelope, seal and write your name and RACV Member number and signature in the space provided on the ballot envelope, and post the reply paid envelope to the Returning Officer.

VOTING CLOSES

All ballot papers must be received by 5.00 p.m. Monday 13 October 2008.

FURTHER INFORMATION

All queries concerning the Election are to be directed to the Election Hotline on 1300 737 880.

From the *RACV* website

What is being said?

1 Definitions: What is the meaning of the following?

a ballot _____

b regardless _____

c eligible _____

d honorary _____

e manufacturers _____

f absentee _____

g invalid _____

h Returning Officer _____

2 What is the purpose of this election? _____

3 How many candidates are to be elected? _____

4 What does the writer mean when he says that a person in love might as well have his brain sealed in a jam jar?

_____

_____

5 Why was Vicki biting her apple so carefully? _____

6 What was Lockie's opinion of the Greenhouse effect? _____

7 What was Vicki trying to talk to Lockie about? _____

_____

8 What was Lockie actually thinking about? _____

_____

9 Why did Vicki say Lockie was useless? _____

_____

10 Why did Lockie think he was useless? _____

_____

11 What did Lockie really mean when he said he was asking a 'hypodermical' question? _____

_____

12 What did Vicki think of marriage? _____

_____

13 How do Vicki's parents feel about each other? _____

_____

14 Why did Vicki say her parents are like politicians? _____

_____

What does it mean?

15 Why do you think Lockie was finding it so difficult to answer Vicki's questions? _____

_____

16 Why might Lockie suddenly have asked Vicki if she would ever have kids? _____

_____

17 Why do you think Vicki was so critical of marriage? _____

_____

What do I think about it?

18 The writer has used many Australian expressions in this book. List four Australian expressions from this passage and explain their meaning.

19 Describe this scene from Vicki's point of view. Write in the first person (I ...) as though you are Vicki. (About 100 words.)

Comprehension
Unit 10
Global warming is a slow drip, drip, drip apocalypse

Rachel Carbonell
The Age

WHETHER IT'S WATER OR MONEY, WE'RE USING MORE THAN WE HAVE

It seems every generation has its own version of the apocalypse. Climate change may be the Armageddon of the new millennium, yet somehow it lacks the menace of, say, an atom bomb. It is destruction by increments. It is hidden in the cracks of a drought. Or a 'water crisis', as we city-dwellers call it.

Farmland turned to salt pans. Water levels so low that if they were exam results they'd be an 'F' for fail.

When I think about it, I breathe faster. And since I had children, that dread has worsened. It keeps me awake at night. And in the morning, I try to scratch some hope out of the dusty ground of fear. Perhaps that's just parenthood. I wonder if everyone feels this wake-in-the-night worry—the big company chiefs, our leaders and decision makers? If so, I see little sign of it. Am I the only one who would welcome harsher water restrictions?

I wish we had recycled water technology pumping away some of my anxiety. I don't care about the so-called 'yuck' factor. My toddler would be happy to slurp the scum off the goldfish pond at this point in her life. I think it's time to harness that lack of prejudice and follow her lead.

This year, I'm planting our first family vegetable garden with my two-year-old. Tomatoes have been popping up under the avocado tree and in the basil pots. And parsley is sprouting from the lawn. We water our seedlings every day. It wouldn't occur to me to fetch the water for gardening from a tap or hose. We use her bathwater, rainwater and the grey river from our washing machine. It's great to be able to teach a child not to waste precious resources and I love her reverence for water. But it makes me sad, too. If my childhood summers could be captured in a sound, it would be a splash.

I take my daughter to the public baths, but the kiddy pool is often shut. So sometimes I break the rules and put a puddle in our plastic clamshell in the backyard on hot days. The problem is that a bit of backyard splashing is not the worst of my sins. Once in a while I accidentally run a huge bath for the kids (when I put too much hot in and create an ocean trying to cool it down). Or I wash my clothes that aren't quite as dirty as they could be. Like tax law, water restrictions are full of loopholes. I may not be breaking the law, but I know I'm doing wrong. I'm watering my garden with the proceeds of my ill-gotten gains.

Occasionally, I imagine an impoverished African mother watching me as I slosh all this water about. It fills me with shame and guilt. I only do it because I can. And when I can't, I won't. But why not stop now? Instead, I fume at the sight of a broken water main gushing unchecked. Or note, bitterly, that the person next to me in the shower at the local pool has taken three times longer than my kid and me combined.

But finding scapegoats doesn't ease the gnawing in my stomach. We had tough times on my family farm when I was a child, too. When our spring-fed dam dried up shortly before the Ash Wednesday bushfires in 1983, my dad dug a new hole next to the old spring and enough water trickled out to get us through that drought. This year that hole almost dried up. And my parents have a new topic to squabble about: how to prioritise what water they have.

My mum, who for so long has sustained both her family and her soul with a big, beautiful vegetable garden, can only plant a few seedlings this summer. Any, despite a recent downpour, extra water still has to be saved for firefighting emergencies. Mum taught me the practicalities and romance of a family garden, something I'm now trying to pass on to my daughter.

My parents have a barometer on the wall of their country property. It's almost an instrument of torture. With big rains finally forecast, the needle pointed to 'Rain' for days, but for a while all they got was a few millimetres. It felt like the universe was straining to squeeze out those few drops.

Lately, water shortages have taken a back seat to the global financial meltdown. But I see no reason to stop worrying. Whether we're talking climate change, water or money, we're using more than we have. I just hope there's a silver lining to all these dark, dry clouds and that the fear will force us to adopt a more sustainable reality.

What is being said?

1 Definitions: what is the meaning of the following?

a apocalypse _____

b Armageddon _____

c millennium _____

d reverence _____

e loophole _____

f scapegoat _____

2 What is 'destruction by increments'? _____

_____

3 What has made the writer dread climate change? _____

_____

4 What does the writer mean by the 'yuck' factor of recycled water? _____

_____

5 Why is the writer sad that her daughter has such a reverence for water? _____

_____

6 How does the writer feel when she flouts the water restrictions? _____

7 Why does the writer describe her parents' barometer as 'an instrument of torture'? _____

_____

_____

8 Which new issue has pushed water shortages from the front pages? _____

_____

What does it mean?

9 The writer uses metaphors to help get her point across to the readers. Explain what each of the following images suggests to the reader:

a 'Climate change may be the new Armaggedon.' _____

_____

_____

b 'I try to scratch some hope from the dusty ground of fear.' _____

_____

_____

c 'I just hope there's a silver lining to all these dark, dry clouds.' _____

_____

_____

What do I think about it?

10 Compose two letters to the editor of the newspaper, replying to this article. One letter should agree with the author's sentiments, the other should disagree.

Comprehension

A newspaper is made up of many different sections. Here is a glossary of terms that are used to describe the different sections of a newspaper.

ADVERTISEMENTS

These help pay for the production of the paper. Advertisers must make sure that their product will be of interest to the readers of a particular paper.

BUSINESS NEWS

This consists of reports of activities in the business world, such as a company takeover or the bankruptcy of a large business.

CLASSIFIED ADVERTISEMENTS

These small advertisements may be telling people about a birth, death or marriage or they may be trying to sell something (e.g. a car or a house) or they may be advertising a job vacancy.

COMICS

Most papers contain a section where various regular comic strips appear. These provide a bit of entertainment to offset the often depressing news of the day.

CROSSWORDS

Another section to provide light relief. Some crosswords are simple, others are cryptic and more difficult.

EDITORIAL

The opinion of the editor (and often the senior journalists) on a current news issue.

INDEX OR CONTENTS

This is generally located near the start of the paper and tells you on which page to find various sections of the paper.

LETTERS TO THE EDITOR

These are written to the editor by readers wishing to comment on an issue in the news.

NEWS REPORT (LOCAL)

This is a report of an event that has happened in the local neighbourhood and which will be of interest to people living there.

NEWS REPORT (NATIONAL)

This is a report of an important event that has happened in Australia.

NEWS REPORT (WORLD)

This is a report of an important event that has happened somewhere else in the world.

PHOTO STORY

This is an item in which the photograph tells the story and is generally accompanied by a two- or three-line caption.

POLITICAL CARTOON

This is a cartoon that makes fun of some aspect of current politics.

SPORTS NEWS

A report on a sporting event that has recently taken place or a story about a sporting personality.

STOCK EXCHANGE REPORT

A report of the day's trading on the stock market that tells the reader which shares have gained or lost in value.

TV GUIDE

Details of programs to be shown on TV during the coming week.

TV REVIEW

A review of a recent TV show. The reviewer gives a brief description of the show and a personal opinion of it.

WEATHER FORECAST

This is a report on weather conditions for the next few days. It often includes graphs and maps.

What is being said?

1 Definitions: what is the meaning of the following?

a glossary _____

b takeover _____

c bankruptcy _____

d job vacancy _____

e   offset _____

f   cryptic crossword _____

g   caption _____

2 Why do papers contain advertisements? _____

_____

3 Give one example of business news. _____

4 Give five examples of advertisements that can be found in the classified advertisements. _____

_____

_____

5 Why do papers include comics? _____

_____

6 Who usually writes the editorial? _____

7 Where would you usually find the index? _____

8 What are the three different types of news reports? _____

_____

9 What is the function of a political cartoon? _____

_____

10 What would you find in the Stock Exchange report? _____

_____

11 How does a TV review differ from a TV guide? _____

_____

Comprehension

What does it mean?

12 Why must advertisers make sure their product will be of interest to the readers of a particular paper?

_____

_____

_____

13 In your own words, explain the difference between an editorial and a letter to the editor. _____

_____

_____

_____

What do I think about it?

14 Make up a classified advertisement for a house, a car or a horse. Try to make it sound appealing to
    potential buyers. (About 100 words.)

Comprehension
Unit 12
Dog days a delight

Herald Sun

COMEDY

Marley and Me

(111 MINUTES, PG)

★ ★ ★½

The players: Owen Wilson, Jennifer Aniston, Alan Arkin, Eric Dane, Kathleen Turner

Behind the scenes: Directed by David Frankel, based on a book by John Grogan

The plot: Marley, a dog that lives life to the fullest and is loved by his family in spite of his infuriating disobedience, provides ample material for a newspaper columnist.

In short: Paws for thought

For a comedy about a dog with boundless energy and *joie de vivre*, you need a good supply of tissues to survive *Marley and Me*.

The publicity girls were blubbering like babies, and loving it.

For the hardened critic, it's one thing to be jotting notes in a dark cinema, leaking eyes is just another challenge.

Seriously, labelling this a weepie is no criticism. It proves the film's success that we become so fond of the Grogan family of Palm Beach, Florida, that their joy is our joy, their worries are ours and their sorrows shoot a bolt through our sentimental hearts.

For the most part, *Marley and Me* is very funny.

The Marley of the title, named for reggae superstar Bob Marley, is a boisterous Labrador retriever whose 13 years of life are tracked from cute-bundle-of-puppy-fun to creaky old canine.

He's John and Jennifer Grogan's practice baby, adopted from a shelter before they commit to having children.

Colleague Sebastian (Eric Dane) convinces John with: 'If you have a dog, you're a master. You feed 'em, you walk 'em, you let them out every now and then. A Labrador is supposed to be like kids, only easier to train.'

Famous last words!

Marley is so naughty, his behaviour is often more horrifying than hilarious.

He chews furniture, pillows, flooring, and anything left lying around or not put safely away. He drinks out of the toilet and eats a gold necklace (retrieved and washed) and an answering machine.

Walking him is like trying to harness a hurricane. People at the beach and in their neat neighbourhood are appalled. He can't be left alone, or with a sitter.

Beyond redemption, he's kicked out of dog-obedience school and John is berated by the trainer, a dishevelled Ms Kornblutt (Kathleen Turner).

So why does the Grogan family keep him? Because he is a member of the Grogan family. He stands for unconditional love and belonging.

This film springs from the unlikely source of *Sun-Sentinel* newspaper columns by journalist John Grogan, later republished as an autobiography.

Alan Arkin is adorable as the dry-witted mentor and editor who tosses John—an aspiring front-line news reporter—into the role as a columnist that eventually sees him become a regional treasure.

Owen Wilson and Jennifer Aniston have the right chemistry to convince us from the moment they appear as newlyweds, through the ups and downs in their marriage, careers, home life and in raising three children.

Over the years of blessings and disappointments Marley is their personal challenge, their companion and their resident comedian.

His antics and disasters make handy source material for John, whose columns gradually grow into a potted family history.

Young children might be ruled out of viewing the film by its sexual content, all in the line of pregnancy duty, and there are raw times and marital rows that have a strong ring of pain.

Though the film is too long, it consistently holds your attention with a meaningful script and a playful, though not goofy, approach.

Take the children. Take the tissues. Sit. Stay.

What is being said?

1 Definitions: what is the meaning of the following?

a boundless _____

b joie de vivre _____

c weepie _____

d sentimental _____

e reggae _____

f redemption _____

g berated _____

h ample _____

2 How did Marley get his name? _____

3 How many years of Marley's life are covered in this film? _____

4 List three examples of Marley's bad behaviour. _____

_____

5 How did *Marley and Me* come to be a film? _____

_____

6 Who plays the role of the dog trainer in the film? _____

7 Who directed the film? _____

8 Why do John and Jennifer Grogan decide to get a dog? _____

_____

9 What language device is 'Dog days a delight' an example of? _____

What does it mean?

10 Why, according to the review, might *Marley and Me* be unsuitable for young children? _____

_____

_____

11 A *pun* is a play on words. Explain the pun in the expression 'Paws for thought'. _____

_____

12 Explain the humour in, 'Take the children. Take the tissues. Sit. Stay'. _____

_____

_____

What do I think about it?

13 Either:

- Write a short review of a film you have enjoyed. You should try to include an alliterative headline and include a brief description of the plot, your opinion of the film and reasons for holding that opinion. Try to include some humour and a pun.

  or

- Write a short description of a difficult pet you have owned.

Comprehension
Unit 13
Three dead in first seven hours of the year

Jason Dowling
The Age

Victoria's road toll has had its worst start to the year in a decade and police have warned that drivers talking on mobile phones will be targeted this year along with the 10 most dangerous accident areas.

Three people were killed in the first seven hours of 2009—the worst start to a new year since 1997. The first was a bare-chested male motorcyclist not wearing a helmet, killed on St Kilda's Beaconsfield Parade.

The horror start followed Victoria's lowest road toll on record, with 304 people killed in 2008, 28 fewer than in 2007.

The other three deaths yesterday included another motorcyclist, in his 20s, killed on the Princes Highway near Bairnsdale, and two men aged in their 20s killed in a single-car accident near Geelong.

Victoria's Christmas holiday toll stands at 16. The national toll is at 54.

Accident experts said the next battle would be to reduce the state's road toll below 300.

The 2008 result was largely due to a significant reduction in fatalities in the last three months of the year, with the lowest number of fatalities in December since 1952. The end-of-year drop coincided with increased police activity.

Assistant Commissioner Ken Lay said this year there would be a crackdown on specific local government areas with high accident levels.

'Half the fatalities in this state sit within 10 local government areas, so we will be focusing our efforts on those 10 areas during 2009,' he said.

The City of Melbourne accounts for the highest number of road trauma cases. Other hot spots are Boroondara, Casey, Kingston, Brimbank, Dandenong, Geelong, Monash, Mornington Peninsula and Frankston.

Mr Lay said an increase in pedestrian deaths and accidents caused by 'driver distractions' such as mobile phones, would also be targeted this year.

'The pedestrian issue has been a major problem for us. One of the worrying things about pedestrians [killed] is nearly half of them are people over the age of 65,' he said. Almost one in five people killed on Victoria's roads last year were pedestrians.

Mr Lay said too many people were talking on phones while driving.

'In recent times we have seen two tragic deaths that are directly attributable to people using mobile phones—so this distraction is certainly a growing issue for us,' he said.

Road minister Tim Pallas said there would be no 'triumphalism' following the record low toll. 'It is absolutely important that we continue to drive the road toll down,' he said.

Road safety experts said lowering speed limits, safer cars and tougher enforcement could help reduce the toll to below 300.

The senior research fellow at Monash University's Accident Centre, Bruce Corben, said speed limits had to be reduced in many areas.

'I think we need to look at our whole urban setting and the sorts of travel speeds and speed limits that we have —we are at least 10, sometimes 20 km/h higher than comparable countries in Europe and North America,' he said.

RACV public policy manager Brian Negus said more could be done to prevent drink-drivers reoffending. 'A lot of this is about the psychological attitude,' he said. 'I think educational and psychological based testing does need to be further investigated.'

The Government is aiming for a 30 per cent reduction in fatalities by 2017—down to 237.

State Opposition transport spokesman Terry Mulder said more had to be done to increase level-crossing safety and reduce pedestrian deaths.

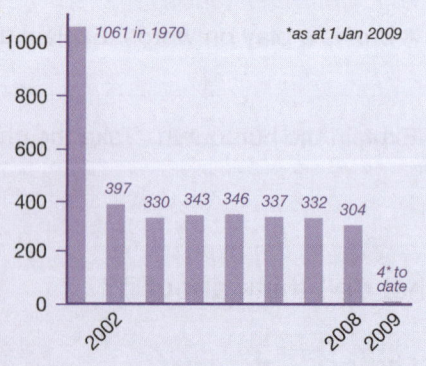

NUMBER OF DEATHS

1061 in 1970   *as at 1 Jan 2009

What is being said?

1 Definitions: what is the meaning of the following?

a road trauma _____

b attributable _____

    c triumphalism _____

    d enforcement _____

    e urban area _____

2 What has prompted this article? _____

3 Describe the first person killed in 2009. _____

4 In which year was Victoria's lowest road toll? _____

5 What is suggested as the cause of the drop in fatalities in the last three months of 2008?

_____

6 Why will the police focus on ten specific local government areas in 2009? _____

_____

7 What is worrying Ken Lay about the increase in pedestrian deaths? _____

_____

8 Who is Bruce Corben? What is his suggestion to help lower the road toll? _____

_____

_____

9 What position does Brian Negus hold? What action does he advocate to prevent drink-drivers reoffending?

_____

_____

10 What is the Government's target for a reduction in fatalities by 2017? _____

What does it mean?

11 Which of the persuasive techniques do you find most effective: the statistics and comments from 'experts' in the article or the graph? Give reasons for your answer.

_____

_____

_____

_____

12 What is the purpose of this article? _____

_____

_____

What do I think about it?

13 Devise a new headline for this article. _____

_____

14 Write a letter to the editor of a daily newspaper giving your suggestion for lowering the road toll.

Fay Burstin
Herald Sun

The 'caveman diet' concept of eating unprocessed natural foods has been gathering momentum in recent years.

Its popularity has been spurred on by star followers such as actors Demi Moore and Halle Berry.

But a bold new theory presents the most convincing evidence yet that modern chronic illness including obesity, diabetes and heart disease are caused by our rapidly evolving food supply colliding with our ancient genes.

Research by eight internationally renowned nutrition and anthropology experts, including two leading Australians, claims our slowly evolving bodies haven't been able to keep up with our fast changing diets and lifestyles.

'Modern humans are still based genetically on the dietary pattern our hunter-gatherer ancestors survived on millions of years ago,' said co-author Associate Professor Neil Mann from RMIT University.

'Yet just 10 000 years ago, in our more recent past, the arrival of agriculture shifted our diet away from lean meat and plants that were low in fat and high in protein, vitamins and minerals.

'And our genetic make-up hasn't had time to adjust.'

The findings, published recently in the *American Journal of Clinical Nutrition,* identify seven major nutritional differences between the modern Western diet and that of our ancestors, which the authors claim underlie the dramatic rise in disease:

1 GLYCAEMIC LOAD
The blood glucose-raising potential of our diet has risen, increasing the risk of insulin resistance, obesity and type 2 diabetes.

2 TYPE OF FAT CONSUMED
We eat less omega-3 and more omega-6 saturated fatty acids, known to increase risk of heart, inflammatory and auto-immune diseases.

3 MACRONUTRIENT COMPOSITION
We eat more carbohydrates, which also increase the glycaemic load, at the expense of protein, which can protect our hearts and benefit cholesterol levels.

4 MICRONUTRIENT DENSITY
We have a much lower concentration of vitamins and minerals in favour of nutrient-dense, highly refined foods.

5 ACID-BASE BALANCE
Our diet is now tilted in favour of unhealthy acids.

6 SODIUM/POTASSIUM RATIO
A huge 400 per cent increase in salt intake has completely reversed the delicate sodium/potassium balance, affecting our cells and body fluids, possibly leading to stroke, gastrointestinal tract cancers and other ailments.

7 FIBRE CONTENT
Fibre has been substantially reduced in favour of refined cereals with empty calories.

Professor Mann said that the argument that dietary factors caused or exacerbated virtually all diseases of modern civilisation was multilayered, with seven fundamental shifts interwoven.

'Rather than perceiving single dietary elements as causes of modern chronic diseases, such as high salt intake causing high blood pressure, a more complex picture is presented,' he said.

But the take-home messages were disarmingly simple and common sense.

'Eat simple, unrefined foods similar to those humans have eaten since the dawn of time,' Prof Mann said.

'As Australians, we should be making use of our access to good quality fruit, vegetables, fish and lean red meat.'

What is being said?

1 Definitions: what is the meaning of the following?

a   unprocessed _____

b   chronic _____

c   anthropology _____

d   inflammatory _____

e   auto-immune diseases _____

f   gastrointestinal _____

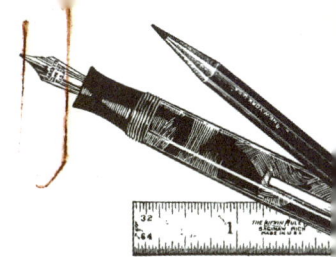

g ailments _____

h exacerbated _____

i unrefined _____

2 What did the 'caveman diet' consist of? _____

3 Which backgrounds were the eight international experts drawn from? _____

_____

4 What, according to the researchers, is the result of us eating more carbohydrates than our Stone Age ancestors?

_____

_____

5 What has happened to our intake of fat? _____

_____

6 What is the potential effect of this on our health? _____

_____

7 How much more salt do we consume today compared to our Stone Age ancestors? _____

_____

8 According to the study, what are the health risks associated with this increased salt intake?

_____

_____

What does it mean?

9 In your own words, summarise the findings of this research. _____

_____

_____

10 Summarise the key features of the modern Western diet. _____

_____

_____

11 How do the researchers know what cavemen ate? _____

_____

What do I think about it?

12 Design a healthy and appetising day's menu for yourself based on the findings of this study.

13 Imagine that you are the creative director of an advertising agency which has been given the job of designing a television advertisement highlighting the health benefits of the 'caveman' diet. Divide a page into two columns. The first column should be headed 'visuals'. This includes what the viewer will see and the camera shots to be used. The second column should be headed 'audio' and it will include what the viewer will hear as well as the script. Make sure that you come up with a slogan for this healthy way of eating.

Comprehension
Unit 15
Flour Babies

'I'm sorry, Simon, but I have no choice. If you don't have a reason to be out of class, I'm forced to give you a detention.'

'It will have to be Monday week,' Simon warned her. 'I'm fully booked till then.'

'Oh, Simon!' said Miss Arnott, pressing the points on her temple where her headaches always started.

'It's all right,' Simon assured her valiantly. 'I don't mind.' And it was true. Between trying to explain, and taking another detention, he much preferred the detention. It was easier.

'Monday week, then.'

Like an unseasonal Santa, Simon nodded, gripped the bin bag, and moved off grimly down the corridor. Miss Arnott stepped aside to let him pass.

And saw the trail of flour.

'Simon—'

'Yes, Miss Arnott?'

But she had gone, fleeing to the staffroom to get some water for her aspirins. Simon stood looking at her footprints down the flour. Something—call it prescience, call it second sight—warned him Miss Arnott wouldn't be with them very much longer. The woman was losing her grip, that was quite obvious. And if there was one thing you needed to be a teacher, it was grip. You needed it from a quarter past eight in the morning till a quarter past four at night. He stopped to count the hours on his fingers. Eight. It sounded a major grind, but, when you came to think, it was only a third of each day. Eight measly hours. If poor Miss Arnott couldn't even manage that, then she'd better not leave and have a baby.

Now there was a real job, thought Simon. Twenty-four hour shifts. Every day. For nearly twenty years. No breaks. No holidays. It made one of Hyacinth's parties look like a mayfly's quick blink. Being a parent was pretty well a life sentence. Why, if instead of going off to hospital to have a baby all those years ago, his mother had stabbed someone to death with a bread knife, she'd be out of gaol by now. Twice over, probably, if she'd been good.

From the novel *Flour Babies* by Anne Fine

What is being said?

1 Definitions: what is the meaning of the following?

a temple _____

b valiantly _____

c unseasonal Santa _____

d grimly _____

e fleeing _____

f prescience _____

g measly _____

h mayfly _____

2 Why was Miss Arnott forced to give Simon a detention? _____

_____

3 Why couldn't Simon attend Miss Arnott's detention until Monday week? _____

_____

4 Why did Miss Arnott press her temple? _____

_____

5 Why did Simon prefer detentions to explaining? _____

6 Simon was holding a bag of flour, which he had to look after like a baby for a class project. Why did he look like an 'unseasonal Santa'?

_____

7 What did Miss Arnott do when she saw the trail of flour? _____

_____

8 Why did Simon think Miss Arnott wouldn't be teaching them much longer? _____

_____

9 What quality did Simon think a teacher needed? _____

10 Why did Simon think having a baby was a real job? _____

_____

_____

What does it mean?

11 How did Simon react to Miss Arnott? _____

_____

_____

_____

12 How did Miss Arnott cope with Simon's absence from class? _____

_____

_____

_____

13 Explain why Simon thought his mother would have a lighter sentence for murder than having a baby?

_____

_____

_____

_____

What do I think about it?

14 Describe this incident from the point of view of Miss Arnott. Write in the first person (I ...) as though you are Miss Arnott.

15 'Being a parent was pretty well a life sentence.' Do you agree with this statement? Give reasons for your answer. (At least 100 words.)

Comprehension

Comprehension
Unit 16
Horoscope

The Age

ARIES
Mar 21–Apr 20

Many of you can expect a surprise occurrence in a love relationship. Some of you could be smitten by falling in love at first sight today.

TAURUS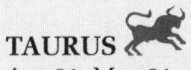
Apr 21–May 21

Something unusual might take place today, at home or with a family member, possibly having to do with art or romance. The course of true love never runs smooth—it hiccups.

GEMINI
May 22–Jun 21

Whatever you do today, especially for fun, will be exciting, original and certainly a break from your normal routine. Since you hate to be bored, this could be a welcome diversion.

CANCER
Jun 22–Jul 23

It is highly likely that you will have an unusual expenditure today, or a surprise connected with your finances and your banking. This could be an opportunity to purchase something unique.

LEO
Jul 24–Aug 23

You seem to be looking for something different and exciting today. If you are in a committed relationship, do not be led astray by a mere bonbon.

VIRGO
Aug 24–Sept 23

Expect the unexpected at work today. This does not have to be something terrible or bothersome; it could be an offer of help from a secret source that surprises you.

LIBRA
Sept 24–Oct 23

Unusual people—those you consider to be characters—hold a special appeal for you today. Because of this, you will likely talk to someone who is different from you.

SCORPIO
Oct 24–Nov 22

A boss might catch you off guard today by doing or saying something quite unexpected. Whenever this happens, it's an opportunity for you to realise that you never really know someone, even if you think you do.

SAGITTARIUS
Nov 23–Dec 21

Expect a quick and sudden opportunity to travel or study today. Your ability to respond is a minor test of your flexibility right now.

CAPRICORN
Dec 22–Jan 20

You might suddenly receive a gift, inheritance or benefit that is something quite out of the blue. If this is the case, make sure that, in some way or other, you pass the favour on.

AQUARIUS
Jan 21–Feb 19

Your partner might say or do something today that could upset you or, at the very least, surprise you. You are advised to think before you act.

PISCES
Feb 20–Mar 20

Something attractive or beautiful might be introduced to your work space today. Free your mind of rigid expectations and concepts, and be open to new ways of doing things.

What is being said?

1 Definitions: what is the meaning of the following?

a horoscope _____

b smitten _____

c diversions _____

d expenditure _____

e bonbon _____

f bothersome _____

g out of the blue _____

h rigid _____

2 What should Virgos expect today? _____

3 What kind of people will Librans be attracted to today? _____

4 What should Sagittarians expect? _____

_____

5 What are the dates for the sign of Gemini? _____

6 What is the symbol that represents Cancer? _____

7 Which star sign might be caught off guard by their boss today? _____

8 What might happen to Capricorns? _____

_____

9 What sign represents Libra? _____

10 What advice is offered to Pisces? _____

_____

What does it mean?

11 There is a common idea running through most of the star signs for this day. Can you work out what it is?

_____

_____

12 What does the saying 'the course of true love never runs smooth—it hiccups' mean? _____

_____

13 What do you think the advice 'do not be led astray by a mere bonbon' means? _____

_____

14 Some of the advice given about various star signs gives us a hint about the personalities associated with them. What do the following pieces of advice tell us about these signs?

a *Aquarius:* 'you are advised to think before you act.' _____

_____

b *Pisces:* 'free your mind of rigid expectations ... and be open to new ways of doing things.' _____

_____

c *Virgo:* 'expect the unexpected at work today. This does not have to be something terrible or bothersome.' _____

_____

What do I think about it?

15 Imagine that you write the horoscopes. Your theme for the day is 'be prepared'. Write entries for Aquarius, Pisces and Virgo.

Comprehension
Unit 17
Great Expectations

> ### Chapter 1
>
> My father's family name being Pirrip, and my christian name Philip, my infant tongue could make of both names nothing longer or more explicit than Pip. So, I called myself Pip, and came to be called Pip.
>
> I give Pirrip as my father's family name, on the authority of his tombstone and my sister—Mrs Joe Gargery, who married the blacksmith. As I never saw my father or my mother, and never saw any likeness of either of them (for their days were long before the days of photographs), my first fancies regarding what they were like, were unreasonably derived from their tombstones. The shape of the letters on my father's, gave me an odd idea that he was a square, stout, dark man, with curly black hair. From the character and turn of the inscription, '*Also Georgiana Wife of the Above,*' I drew a childish conclusion that my mother was freckled and sickly. To five little stone lozenges, each about a foot and a half long, which were arranged in a neat row beside their grave, and were sacred to the memory of five little brothers of mine—who gave up trying to get a living, exceedingly early in that universal struggle—I am indebted for a belief I religiously entertained that they had all been born on their backs with their hands in their trousers-pockets, and had never taken them out in this state of existence.
>
> Ours was the marsh country, down by the river, within, as the river wound, twenty miles of the sea. My first most vivid and broad impression of the identity of things, seems to be to have been gained on a memorable raw afternoon towards evening. At such a time I found out for certain, that this bleak place overgrown with nettles was the churchyard; and that Philip Pirrip, late of this parish, and also Georgiana wife of the above, were dead and buried; and that Alexander, Bartholomew, Abraham, Tobias, and Roger, infant children of the aforesaid, were also dead and buried; and that the dark flat wilderness beyond the churchyard, intersected with dykes and mounds and gates, with scattered cattle feeding on it, was the marshes; and that the low leaden line beyond, was the river; and that the distant savage lair from which the wind was rushing, was the sea; and that the small bundle of shivers growing afraid of it all and beginning to cry, was Pip.
>
> From the novel *Great Expectations* by Charles Dickens

What is being said?

1 Definitions: what is the meaning of the following?

a explicit _____

b tombstone _____

c derived _____

d inscription _____

e lozenges _____

f sacred _____

g indebted _____

h marsh _____

i raw _____

j bleak _____

k nettles _____

l dykes _____

m lair _____

2 Why did the writer call himself Pip? _____

3 Why does Pip give *Pirrip* as his father's family name? _____

_____

4 Where did Pip get his ideas about the appearance of his deceased parents? _____

_____

5 Why did Pip think his father was a square man? _____

_____

6 Why did Pip think his mother was freckled and sickly? _____

_____

7 How many of Pip's brothers were in the graveyard? _____

8 Why did he think of his baby brothers as lying on their backs with their hands in their pockets? _____

_____

9 What was the weather like when Pip gained his first impression of the identity of things? _____

_____

10 What was the churchyard like? _____

_____

11 What are the names of Pip's deceased brothers? _____

_____

12 What were the marshes? _____

_____

13 How does Pip describe the sea? _____

_____

14 How was Pip feeling at this time? _____

_____

What does it mean?

15 How might the reader realise that this book was first published in 1860? _____

_____

16 What sort of boy does Pip seem to be? _____

_____

_____

What do I think about it?

17 This is the opening of a very famous novel by Charles Dickens. Write your own opening paragraph of a novel, describing one of your first memories. (About 100 words.)

Amanda Ford
Elizabeth Haywood

Part 4
Writing

This section contains 17 double-page units that will help students to develop their writing skills. Students are exposed to a variety of writing techniques, such as point of view, narrative structure, vocabulary building and literary conventions. It covers a range of fiction and non-fiction text-types, including informative, narrative, descriptive, instructional and persuasive, and it explores forms such as biography, reports, newspaper writing, myth, fable and science fiction. The emphasis is on providing different techniques of writing, helping students to improve their written expression and develop writing skills specific to particular genres.

Each unit consists of an interesting and relevant model of writing or graphic stimulus, an explanation of the technique or characteristic of the text type or genre, and space for student responses. The responses will consist of both short answers and more sustained pieces of writing. Activities to be completed off the page are indicated by  .

Writing
Unit 1
Different ways of planning

In this unit and the one that follows, we will be looking at some of the main ways in which writers **plan** their work.

Let's assume that your teacher has given you one or more specific topics to write about. Here are three ways in which you could approach this task:

Brainstorming the topic

Think of anything connected with the topic and write it down. This is a good exercise to do with your classmates, as you will get more ideas from pooling your thoughts.

Approaching the topic logically

Some people prefer to tell the whole story in order from the start. You could write down a list of events in order and then expand them into paragraphs.

Organise your ideas in graphic form

There are many ways of using diagrams and drawings to plan your writing and this method appeals to people who work visually. You could use pieces of paper or cardboard with ideas or points you want to make and arrange them on the table with arrows connecting them, to show the connections. Here is an example:

MY DISASTROUS FIRST ATTEMPT AT SKIING

Excited to be going skiing

Boring bus trip to the snow	Accident after the first ski run	A week in hospital

NEVER AGAIN

---

1 **Brainstorm some ideas for each of the following topics. Ask your classmates for ideas. You should end up with at least four different ways of using each topic.**

a The day my aunt came to live with us _____

_____

_____

_____

b My favourite television show _____

_____

_____

_____

c I felt my bike skidding in the gravel … _____

_____

_____

_____

d Why I love my pet _____

_____

_____

_____

_____

e Don't go in there! _____

_____

_____

_____

_____

2 List four possible points (in order) that could be expanded into paragraphs for the following topics.

    a My day at the snow

       i _____

      ii _____

     iii _____

     iv _____

    b I was left alone in the deserted shopping centre

       i _____

      ii _____

     iii _____

     iv _____

    c Alien invasion

       i _____

      ii _____

     iii _____

     iv _____

3 Draw a diagram to help you plan a piece of writing about a funny experience that you have had.

4 Ask some of your friends how they get ideas for writing and how they plan their work. You may be surprised at the different methods people use to get under way.

Writing

Writing
Unit 2
Finding your own ideas for writing

Sometimes you will be asked to think of your **own ideas for writing**. Writers have many ways of collecting ideas. Here are some of them:

Events from your life
Your life is what you know best. You could write about a birth or a death, a special holiday or your relatives, for example.

Something you have read about or seen on television
You could turn an episode of *The Simpsons* into a story about your life. Or you might have read about a tragedy in the newspaper and you could imagine what it would have been like to be there.

Eavesdropping
You might overhear a conversation on the train or at the shopping centre and use these words as the starting point for a story of your own, for example:

'I couldn't believe she had bought the same shoes as me!'

This could be a story about two friends who have a fight over some shoes. Do they become friends again, or are they enemies forever?

A special place
You could describe a place that is special for you—such as your favourite beach or even your bedroom—and try to explain why you like it so much. It could be connected with a special event in your life.

A photograph
You might decide to tell the story behind a photograph, or you could use it as the starting point for an imaginary story.

Your imagination
Some people have very vivid imaginations and can make up stories that sound exciting and interesting (a good example is the *Lord of the Rings* trilogy). You might have some ideas for a fantasy story that you could discuss with your friends or your teacher.

The units that follow describe many different forms of writing, giving you the tools to develop your ideas in a variety of ways. At a later date, you could look back at these planning units to help you develop the ideas you have thought of into finished pieces of writing.

1   List three important events from your life that you could write about:

a   _____

b   _____

c   _____

2   List three incidents, characters or storylines that you have read about or seen on television that you could use for a story of your own

a   _____
    _____

b   _____
    _____

c   _____

Writing

3   What sort of story could emerge from the following snippets of conversation?

a   'Look out! He's coming this way. Don't let him see you.' _____

_____

_____

_____

b   'Mum said I'm not allowed to go to the movies. I'll show her …' _____

_____

_____

_____

c   'I saw the bike I'm going to get when I turn 14. I just need to find the money.' _____

_____

_____

_____

4   List three special places that you think you could write about.

a   _____

b   _____

c   _____

5   Describe a photograph that you might use as the starting point for a piece of writing. _____

_____

_____

_____

6   List two ideas that could be expanded into a fantasy story.

a   _____

_____

_____

b   _____

_____

_____

7   Think about your favourite stories. Where do you think the authors got their ideas from?

Writing
Unit 3
Audience, purpose and title

Audience and purpose

When you choose a topic you need to decide what your **audience** and **purpose** will be. In other words, *why* are you writing this piece and *for whom*? This will help you to be much more focused in your writing and to make some important decisions about the form in which you choose to write. If, for example, you intended to inform an older audience about skateboarding, you would probably need to provide a **glossary** (word list) of technical terms.

You should attach a **statement of intention**, which outlines your purpose, audience and any other decisions about the way you have chosen to write.

Read the following statement of intention:

Reign of terror

This is a personal piece, based on an actual time in my childhood. I have attempted to capture how terrified we were of our neighbour's dog. I am writing for an audience of younger children so that they realise that fears like this lessen as we grow older. I have chosen to tell my story in a diary format so that the audience will feel that the events are happening as they read.

By Katie

Title

You need to give your writing an interesting and exciting **title**. Avoid boring titles such as 'My holiday' or 'Film review'. Your title could sum up an important idea in your writing or you could use a line from what you have written. It should be interesting enough to make the reader want to read your piece. You should try to develop what is called a **working title** before you start, to help you focus. If you think of something better when you finish, you can change your title. Katie's title, 'Reign of terror', is much more intriguing than 'The dog next door' would have been.

Revision

The next important aspect of presentation is making your writing as good as it can be. There are three stages to this process:

- The first stage asks you to look for ways of improving your writing (**revision**).
- The second stage asks you to find your mistakes and correct them (**proofreading**).
- The third stage asks you to look at ways of presenting your work as attractively as possible (**presentation**).

---

1 a What is Katie's purpose? _____

_____

b Who is her audience? _____

c In which form has she chosen to tell her story? _____

2 a Devise an exciting title for each of the following:

i a review of the film *Where the Wild Things Are* _____

_____

ii an editorial that argues pit bull terriers should be banned _____

_____

b Think of an alternative title for a novel that you have read or studied this year. Explain why you think this would be a good title.

_____

_____

_____

_____

_____

3 Take a piece of writing that you have completed recently, reread it (preferably aloud), and ask yourself the following questions. Then rewrite the piece of writing and hand it in to your teacher, together with the original piece and your written answers to the questions.

a How can I improve my writing? (**Revision**)

  i Does it make sense?

  ii How could I change it so that it sounds better?

  iii Does it need more explanation anywhere? (For example, about characters/ actions/ideas/opinions/setting?)

  iv Could I use better words to keep the reader interested all the way through?

  v Have I succeeded in writing effectively for my purpose and audience? (For example, is the language level appropriate?)

  vi Have I used a particular word or words too often? (For example, should I make greater use of pronouns rather than using a noun all the time?)

  vii Am I using past, present and future tenses correctly?

  viii Should I have joined some short sentences to make longer sentences using conjunctions?

b How can I find my mistakes and correct them? (**Proofreading**)

  i Have I left out any words?

  ii Does my punctuation seem to be correct? (For example, have I used commas, full stops, question marks and apostrophes when I should? Have I used quotation marks when people speak in my stories? Have I started a new line for each speaker?)

  iii Have I checked the spelling of any words that I am not sure of?

c How will I present my work attractively? (**Presentation**)

  i Have I used clear titles, headings and subheadings when necessary?

  ii Have I taken care to write neatly, or type my work? When I type, have I made use of bold and italics when appropriate?

  iii Have I set out my work attractively on the page? (For example, using borders and illustrations.)

Writing
Unit 4
CD and website reviews

Although film and book reviews are probably the most common, there are many different kinds of review. All should include some information about the content of the product and some comment or opinion on its success or failure.

CD reviews
An example of a **CD review** follows.

> **Guy Sebastian: Like it Like That [Sony]**
>
> Guy Sebastian is back and better than ever, following up the success of his Aria-topping single, 'Like it Like That', with an album that will end any one-hit wonder aspersions. Guy's love of R&B has influenced these songs, making it the feel-good album of summer. Showing just how far Guy's come, John Mayer (Jennifer Aniston's musician ex) plays guitar and sings back-up vocals on several tracks. He's not only our first Australian Idol winner, but this album proves he remains our best.
> For fans of: Mika; Backstreet Boys
>
> Wendy Squires
> *Australian Women's Weekly*

Website reviews
To write a **review of a website**, you need to work out what makes a particular website good, for example, is it easy to navigate? Are the graphics clear and quick?

1   Choose a CD that you know well and complete the following. This will help you to develop a plan for writing an actual review of it.

a   Title, artist and label _____

_____

b   Type of music _____

_____

c   Background on this artist and other work by them _____

_____

_____

d   Similar groups or singers for comparison _____

_____

e   Your opinion of the CD, with reasons _____

_____

_____

_____

Writing

f Recommendation _____

_____

_____

2 In pairs, find an example of a CD review in a newspaper, magazine or on the Internet and discuss whether it is effective. Note whether it includes all the points in Exercise 1.

3 Now use the points you have made in Exercise 1 as a basis for planning your review, paragraph by paragraph. What is the logical order for your review? Which aspects do you want to emphasise? (You may find it useful at this stage to refer back to Units 1–6.) Here is one possible way of organising your review:

- Paragraph 1: Title, artist, label and type of music
- Paragraph 2: Background on this artist and other work by them
- Paragraph 3: Similar groups or singers for comparison
- Paragraph 4: Your opinion of the CD (with reasons); why this CD is special
- Paragraph 5: Final comments and recommendation

Write your own paragraph plan here:

- Paragraph 1: _____
- Paragraph 2: _____
- Paragraph 3: _____
- Paragraph 4: _____
- Paragraph 5: _____

4 Now write your full-scale CD review. It should contain at least three paragraphs and be at least 250 words long.

5 Choose one of your favourite websites and develop a checklist of the elements that make it useful and interesting.

Title and URL of website: _____

What makes it interesting and useful?

- _____
- _____
- _____
- _____

6 Now write a review of the website, making sure you include the elements that you have identified in Exercise 5.

Writing

Writing
Unit 5
Menu

Writing an exciting **menu** requires different skills from writing a review. You need to be brief and to use colourful and enticing words that will make the reader want to eat the food that you have described.

The chef has decided what will be on the menu. You will be writing the menu—how will you make the food sound delicious and inviting?

Here is an example:

ENTRÉE

Aromatic pumpkin soup, delicately spiced with nutmeg and cinnamon
Accompanied by freshly baked crusty bread

Plump chicken dumplings simmered in a soy-flavoured broth
A tasty broth that lifts the dumplings into the stratosphere

MAIN COURSE

Pan-seared tuna on a bed of truffle-spiked mashed potato
Accompanied by homemade lemon pickle

The ultimate burger with the lot—a succulent burger, made from local grain-fed beef, on a wholemeal bun
Served with a spicy tomato salsa

DESSERT

Our chef's special sticky-date pudding
Accompanied by homemade vanilla pod ice-cream and thick clotted cream

Chocolate indulgence—rich mud cake with thick chocolate icing
Thick cream and homemade pistachio ice-cream on the side

Menus like this are fairly typical. They make use of many *adjectives* (describing words) to make the meals sound irresistible; for example, the noun *burger* is livened up with the addition of the adjective *ultimate*. This makes it sound special and different from an ordinary burger.

Writing a menu requires you to think about the way you will *describe* the food, as well as making sure that you have *informed* the diners about the *nature* of the food. It is a skill that is important to restaurant owners. As the menu is often the first impression the diner gets of a restaurant, it must be enticing.

A thesaurus will help you to find words to describe food; for example, looking up the word *delicious* could give you the following synonyms: *delectable, delightful, scrumptious, tasty, appetising, luscious.*

1   Fill in the spaces below with the adjectives used in the menu above.

a   _____   _____   soup

b   _____   _____   _____   bread

c   _____   _____   potato

d   _____   _____   beef

e   _____   _____   cream

2 Fill in the spaces below with your own adjectives that make the reader want to eat the food.

a _____ _____ ice-cream

b _____ _____ spring rolls

c _____ _____ bread

d _____ _____ chicken

e _____ _____ chips

3 Using a thesaurus, dictionary or your own knowledge, find three synonyms for the following words.

a rich (food) _____ _____ _____

b broth _____ _____ _____

c spicy _____ _____ _____

d stew _____ _____ _____

e cake _____ _____ _____

4 Write a menu under the headings below. Include detailed descriptions of the food, including any accompaniments such as sauces or vegetables. (Only include one selection for each section of the menu.)

Entrée

_____
_____
_____

_____

Main course

_____
_____
_____

_____

Dessert

_____
_____
_____

_____

5 Using a suitable computer program, design and print the menu for your new restaurant. You will need a logo and some interesting graphics.

Writing

Writing
Unit 6
Business letters

Sometimes it will be necessary to write a **formal business letter**. Here is an example.

Your address and phone number

6 High Street
Melton
Victoria 3337
Ph. 8888 4444

*Note that all writing starts on the far left of the page; this is called **block form***

Today's date

June 15, 2009

The name and position of the person you are writing to

Ms B Johnson
Personnel Manager
Triumph Architects
22 Finial Street
Melton
Victoria 3337

Dear Ms Johnson,

The body of the letter

I am a Year 9 student at Springfield College. I am writing to enquire about the possibility of doing work experience with your firm. I have always been interested in architecture as a career and many people have mentioned Triumph Architects as a company that is at the cutting edge of the profession. I believe you could help provide me with an excellent insight into the varied applications of architecture today.

'Yours faithfully' is used when the letter begins 'Dear Sir' or 'Dear Madam'

My school has set aside the first two weeks of September for work experience, but if these dates do not suit your firm it may be possible for me to arrange to complete my work experience at another time.

I look forward to hearing from you soon.

Sign your name here

Yours sincerely,

Type your name here

Tom Higgins

After completing your work experience, you should write a **thank you letter** to your employer. Here is an example.

Your address and phone number

6 High Street
Melton
Victoria 3337
Ph. 8888 4444

*Note that all writing starts on the far left of the page; this is called **block form***

Today's date

September 15, 2009

The name and position of the person you are writing to

Ms B Johnson
Personnel Manager
Triumph Architects
22 Finial Street
Melton
Victoria 3337

You might use her first name now

Dear Belinda,

I am writing to thank all of you at Triumph Architects who made my work experience such a rewarding and positive time for me.

The body of the letter

Before working with your team I had no idea of the challenges that the architect faces daily. I am now certain that I want to follow this career path.

Please pass on my special thanks to Nick and Kelly who were never too busy to answer my questions.

I hope to come and visit you soon.

Yours sincerely,

Sign your name here

Type your name here

Tom Higgins

1　Write a letter to a local store (for example, a hardware store, a hairdresser, a clothing store or a sporting goods store) requesting some weekend or after-school work. Set it out like the model letter above:

- The first paragraph should explain who you are and why you would like the job.
- The second paragraph should outline the times you would be available and when you could be contacted for an interview.

2　Write a thank you letter to the local store that has employed you at the weekend for the last year. You are moving to another state and have finished your work at the store.

When you apply for a job, you need to supply a **curriculum vitae**, or **CV**. This is a brief account of your education, qualifications and previous jobs. The words *curriculum vitae* are Latin and mean 'course of life'.

The word **résumé** can be used instead of CV as it has a similar meaning.

You need to be brief and straightforward when writing a CV or résumé. Here is an example:

Curriculum vitae

Name:	Maryanne Smith	**Email:**	msmith@email.com
Address:	6 Smith Road, Smithtown	**Phone:**	9999 9999

Qualifications:
Year 11 Certificate
Bartender's Certificate
Food Handling Certificate
Bronze Medallion (swimming)

Employment history:
Shop assistant, Myer, 2006–2007
Bartender, Smith's Bar, 2008

When you apply for a job, you need to write a **covering letter** that outlines your interest in the particular job you are applying for. This covering letter should indicate your interest in the job and briefly explain why you have applied for it. Here is an example:

Ms Helen Jones
Smith's Café
10 Smith St
Smithtown

Dear Ms Jones

Application for part-time waiting staff

I read your advertisement in the local paper and I wish to apply for one of your positions for part-time waiting staff. I have a Food Handling Certificate and I wish to eventually work in the hospitality industry.

I have good communication skills, as I have demonstrated while I was on Work Experience at your café on the other side of town (names of referees are included below).

I have also learnt how to use your computer ordering system, and I am familiar with the financial software that your chain uses.

My capacity to work both individually and in a team has been demonstrated on Work Experience and when I did some volunteer work with the local food cooperative.

I am able to work flexible hours and I live nearby, so transport will not be a problem.

If given the chance, I believe that I would be a valuable member of the working team at Smith's Café, as I am enthusiastic and have a passion for working with people in a way that can have a positive impact on their lives.

I look forward to hearing from you soon.

Yours faithfully

(sign name here)

Maryanne Smith

1   Plan your CV by filling in your details below. If you have not had any jobs yet, be creative and make some up!

Name: _____

Address: _____

_____

Qualifications: _____

_____

_____

_____

Employment history: _____

_____

_____

_____

_____

_____

2   You are applying for a job as sales assistant at the local surf shop. Fill in the spaces below to help plan your covering letter.

   a   The name and address of the shop and the name of the person you are contacting: _____

   _____

   b   Where you saw the advertisement: _____

   c   Which job you are applying for: _____

   d   Why you are applying for the job (your interest): _____

   _____

   _____

   _____

   e   A reason that you are particularly well suited to the job. (What do you have to offer?):

   _____

   _____

   _____

   _____

3   Write the covering letter based on the information that you have provided in Exercise 2. Set your letter out as shown in the example on the previous page.

Writing
Unit 8
Different forms of writing

> Some writers tell their stories through a **combination** of letters, diaries, emails, made-up newspaper reports, police or psychologists' reports and other material.

1   Why do you think readers might like stories told in these ways? _____

_____

_____

_____

_____

2   As a class, find as many examples as possible of novels and short stories that have been told in different forms and from different points of view. Start by discussing possible examples with your classmates, parents and teachers. You could also interview your school librarians. Write a brief summary of two of these stories using the headings below.

a   i   Title, author and brief plot of story: _____

_____

_____

_____

_____

    ii   Form of writing or point of view: _____

_____

_____

_____

_____

b   i   Title, author and brief plot of story: _____

_____

_____

_____

_____

    ii   Form of writing or point of view: _____

_____

_____

_____

_____

Writing

3　Write a multivoiced story. It should be told through letters, or a combination of letters, diaries and other material. Some possible topics are:

- a problem dog in your street
- a fight
- a man who reported the arrival of a flying saucer in his backyard
- trying to convince your parents why you need more pocket money and a better social life
- a school camp that did not work out very well

Remember to make your different entries show the point of view and personality of each writer. Make sure too that you think about all the people who might have an opinion in relation to the topic you choose. In the case of the school camp, for example, this would include parents, students, teachers, the camp manager, the principal and possibly others. Think about how each would be most likely to express their view—would they use a letter, a report, a diary entry or some other form of writing?

Write your story in the space provided. Alternatively, you could choose to write a longer multivoiced story off the page.

Writing

Writing
Unit 9
Science fiction

Science fiction is the name given to a type of writing (or *genre*) that is based on scientific and technological developments, and makes us think about where these developments might lead our world.

Science fiction looks into the future. Many science-fiction novels, short stories and films turn the reader's (or viewer's) attention to disturbing long-term outcomes of current issues such as pollution or overpopulation. They may take a modern invention or discovery, such as DNA technology, and exaggerate its effect to explore the possible results. In science fiction, many of these discoveries turn out to have a dark side.

The following passage is an extract from a short story titled, 'There Will Come Soft Rains'. It was written in 1950 by Ray Bradbury, a famous science-fiction writer. A nuclear war has left the world empty, but look at what continues to happen in this house:

And then one day the world shook and there was an explosion followed by ten thousand explosions and red fire in the sky and a rain of ashes and radio-activity, and the happy time was over.

In the living room the voice-clock sang, *Tick-tock, seven A.M. o'clock, time to get up!* as if it were afraid nobody would. The house lay empty. The clock talked on into the empty morning.

The kitchen stove sighed and ejected from its warm interior eight eggs, sunny side up, twelve bacon slices, two coffees and two cups of hot cocoa. *Seven nine, breakfast time, seven nine.*

'Today is April 28th, 1985,' said a phonograph voice in the kitchen ceiling. 'Today, remember, is Mr Featherstone's birthday. Insurance, gas, light and water bills are due.'

Somewhere in the walls, relays clicked, memory tapes glided under electric eyes. Recorded voices moved beneath steel needles:

Eight one, run, run, off to school, off to work, run, run, ticktock, eight one o'clock!

But no doors slammed, no carpets took the quick tread of rubber heels. Outside, it was raining. The voice of the weather box on the front door sang quietly: 'Rain, rain, go away, rubbers, raincoats for today.' And the rain tapped on the roof.

At eight thirty the eggs were shrivelled. An aluminium wedge scraped them into the sink, where hot water whirled them down a metal throat which digested and flushed them away to the distant sea.

Nine fifteen, sang the clock, *time to clean.*

From the short story 'There Will Come Soft Rains' by Ray Bradbury

1 **a** Apart from the terrible effects of this war, what aspects of society is Ray Bradbury highlighting for us in this story?

_____

_____

_____

b How accurate do you think Ray Bradbury's predictions have turned out to be? _____

_____

_____

2 **a** Discuss in groups or as a class some examples of science-fiction books that you have read or films that you have seen.

b After your discussion, list two examples. They may be films, novels or short stories.

i _____

ii _____

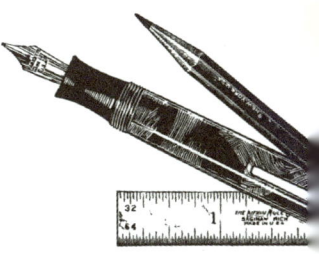

c What were the most important ideas in these films, novels or short stories?

i _____

_____

ii _____

_____

d Did you find that there seemed to be more than one type of science fiction? Explain your answer. _____

_____

_____

_____

_____

_____

_____

_____

_____

_____

3 Now write a science-fiction story. It should be based on what you think a day in your life might be like if you were a teenager living in the year 2105. To help you plan, refer to Unit 1. You might like to write down all the ideas that you could cover and then organise them in the order in which you wish to present them, or you could organise your ideas in a graphic form.

Here are some things that you might cover in your story:

- What are families like in 2105?
- Where do people live?
- What are houses like?
- What kinds of work do people do?
- What do people do in their leisure time?
- Do schools still exist?
- What do students learn?
- Are teachers human or have they been replaced by robots and computers?
- What is fashion like?
- Has the way people have friendships changed?
- What about sport, the environment, discoveries in medicine and science?

Tell your story in the first person. Remember to make your opening as interesting as possible, so that the reader wants to read on and learn more. Try to make the reader think about some particular aspect of life in the future. Will everything be good, or will there be some problems that we need to try to prevent now?

Writing
Unit 10
Play scripts

As you read the following script for a shadow play, the annotations will highlight for you what a **play script** should do.

Note

The curtain is left open throughout the play. A large white sheet is stretched across the stage with a bright light placed behind it. All action (unless otherwise directed) takes place between the light and the sheet. The success of any shadow play lies in the use of visual effects (i.e. clear silhouettes). Players should always move themselves and their props close to the screen to achieve best results.

The setting

Stage directions

Tells actors and the reader where various characters and stage props are located at any time

An operating table is placed behind the sheet. Props used during the operation should be made of cardboard. All of these props should lie flat on the table when not in use. Where possible, sound effects should be pre-taped. This could be done by non-performing members of the troupe with one person in charge of operating the tape during performances.

Scene one

Indicates the entrances and exits of characters

Lionel Lily-Liver and his mother come on stage in front of the white sheet.
(Note: the light behind the white sheet does not come on until the next scene.)

MRS LILY-LIVER   No arguments Lionel—you've had that cold for three days now. I think it's time we got some professional advice.

LIONEL   But mother, this is a hospital. I'm scared of hospitals.

MRS LILY-LIVER   No nonsense now Lionel—nothing to be afraid of. I'm here. And Teddy's here too. Here you are.

(She takes a teddy bear out of her shopping bag and gives it to Lionel.)

Tells actors where to move, what gestures to make and their tone of voice

LIONEL   But I've only got a cold … (He sneezes loudly.)

MRS LILY-LIVER   Oh dear! Emergency! Help! Help!

(The Matron appears. Lionel is in a spasm of coughing. Matron blows a whistle and two attendants run on stage.)

MATRON   (To attendants.) Quickly, before he chokes to death!

(The attendants carry Lionel (and his bear) off-stage. Mrs Lily-Liver is hysterical.)

MRS LILY-LIVER   My poor Lionel, he's never been away from home before!

MATRON   There, there dear. You've nothing to worry about. We're all professional people here. He'll receive the best of care.

(Matron assists Mrs Lily-Liver off-stage.)

Scene two

Describes the kind of lighting required

The light behind the white sheet has been turned on to reveal Lionel being placed on the table by the attendants. Lionel is still spluttering and trying to get down from the table.

Script reproduced with permission of www.enterprisingwords.com

Writing

1 a What kind of person is Lionel's mother? How do you know this? _____

_____

_____

_____

   b When should the light behind the white sheet come on?

_____

   c How does the matron call the two attendants on stage?

_____

2 Take your favourite scene from a novel that your class has worked on this year and turn it into a play script. Think about how you would set up the stage and remember to include instructions about the lighting in your stage directions. Remember, too, to let the actors know how they should speak and move (including entrances and exits).

3 Write a short play of three scenes. Include a cast list (that is, a list of characters with a very brief description of each). For example:

Sanjay. A fourteen-year-old boy.

Rahul. His middle-aged father.

You will also need to include a description of your setting and how the stage will be arranged, for example:

The setting is a dentist's waiting room. Lounge chairs are arranged in a semi-circle at stage left. The receptionist's desk is at the top of stage right, next to it is the entrance and on the back wall of stage left is the dentist's surgery. The lighting is dim until the nurse comes on stage and then a spotlight focuses on her as she bustles around. Some typical waiting-room music begins to play softly.

Next, write the dialogue and stage directions, using the model provided as an example. As in Exercise 2, remember to provide directions about the lighting, entrances and exits, and directions for the characters about how to speak and move.

Choose one of the following topics:

- Dinner in front of the television
- Saturday morning at our place
- Winning
- Everything is so boring around here

Writing
Unit 11
Television scripts

You have seen that play scripts need to provide stage directions that describe how the stage will be set up, what the lighting will be like at various stages of the performance, and how the characters will move and deliver their lines. **Television scripts** need to do all this as well as providing directions about the kinds of camera angles to be used in each shot. These scripts are called *shooting scripts*. Below is a list of terms for the most frequently used camera angles:

- **ECU**: Extreme close-up
- **CU**: Close-up
- **Long shot**: A shot taken from a distance
- **Medium shot**: A shot between a close-up and a long shot
- **Cut**: To go quickly to another shot
- **Zoom**: Movement from a long shot to a close-up
- **Pan**: The camera slowly moves across a scene
- **Soft filter**: Gauze (a very light, transparent fabric) is placed over the camera's lens to soften outlines

Now read through this section of a sample shooting script:

Visual	Audio
We open on an inner-city street late at night (*camera pans across scene*). A teenage boy double-parks, jumps out of the car and runs to the front door of a house (*medium shot*). He looks very upset and pounds on the door (*ECU*).	*Silence, then the sound of a car stopping suddenly, running footsteps and finally the boy pounding on the front door.*
	Tran: 'For God's sake Mum, Dad. Wake up!'
(*Camera cuts to inside the house*) We see Mr Nguyen (Tran's father) pulling on his dressing gown and rushing down the stairs (*medium shot*). He opens the door. (*Camera cuts to Tran.*)	**Tran:** 'It's the café, Dad. It's on fire!'

Soap operas

Most of you probably watch at least one long-running serial on television. Some of these programs are referred to as **soap operas** and they are very popular with viewers.

- *Setting* is very important in soap operas, as the action generally takes place in a limited number of locations, which are used repeatedly.
- The same kinds of *characters* tend to appear in most soap operas; for example, the local gossip, the kind and helpful person, the snob, the young person who has a heart of gold but is always getting into trouble.
- *Storylines* are often quite complicated, with a number of stories involving different characters.
- *Endings* are very important in soap operas because the writers want to keep the audience watching. That is why, at the end of every episode, something dramatic or mysterious happens so that the audience is dying to know what happens next and will tune in to find out.

1 a List three possible reasons for the popularity of soap operas

   i _____

   ii _____

   iii _____

b Describe the setting of two soap operas with which you are familiar.

i _____

_____

ii _____

_____

c Describe two soap opera characters whom you really like and two whom you dislike. Are these characters familiar soap opera types?

i _____

_____

_____

_____

ii _____

_____

_____

_____

d Think about a soap opera episode that you have watched in the last week. Outline the main stories that were being followed in this episode.

_____

_____

_____

_____

_____

e What happened at the ending to make the viewer want to watch the next episode? _____

_____

2 Write a soap opera:
- First, you should prepare an outline describing the setting of your soap opera.
- You will then need to list and describe the characters who will appear in the series. Think carefully about your target audience. If, for example, you are writing for a young audience, you will need to include a lot of young characters.
- Write a brief storyline for the first three episodes and remember to have several storylines involving a number of different characters going at the same time. Outline the way you will finish the first two episodes to make the viewer want to keep watching.
- Finally, write a shooting script for the very start of your first episode.

Newspapers give us more than just the news. The writers (or *journalists* as they are known) also comment on the events and happenings in the community, the nation and the world. The most important page of comment in a newspaper is the editorial page. This page contains the **editorial**, which is intended to give the newspaper's opinion, and letters to the editor from readers who want to express their views. Often the editorial page also contains, or is near to, political cartoons and regular comment columns by senior journalists.

Read the following example of an editorial:

HERALD SUN

BAN THE BIFF

The Victorian Government has made a strong stand against violence in community sport.

Clubs must sign a code of conduct if they are to receive Government subsidies.

While some might complain about over-reguation, it is overdue.

Clubs and sporting organisations have been unable to deal with outbreaks of abuse and violence that have forced football games to be cancelled and led to brawls among spectators.

The new code will cover racial, religious and sexual issues and follows calls by the *Herald Sun* for action to prevent the violence that has seen young players as well as umpires attacked by spectators.

Note three important features of the layout of an editorial:
- The newspaper's banner headline (the name of the newspaper) appears at the top of the editorial.
- It has an attention-grabbing headline.
- The headline may contain a *pun* (a clever or humorous play on the meanings of words), it may make use of *alliteration* (the commencement of two or more closely connected words with the same letter), or it may *sensationalise* or *dramatise* the issue in some way.
- It is often written in a single-column format.

1 a How do you think the headline of the above editorial works to grab the reader's attention? _____

_____

_____

_____

b Editorials express a point of view that is often a call to action. What is the point of view expressed in the editorial?

_____

_____

_____

c Editorials contain a mixture of fact and opinion:

- A *fact* is something that can be proved (for example, *The first car was invented by Karl Benz*)
- An *opinion* is simply someone's belief (for example, *Fords are better than Holdens*)

i List two facts from the editorial. _____

_____

_____

_____

ii List one opinion from the editorial. _____

_____

_____

2 Design an eye-catching headline for editorials on each of the following subjects:

a Water safety _____

_____

b Violence in sport _____

_____

c The problem of litter _____

_____

3 Write an editorial. Remember to format it correctly. Make up a banner headline, write your editorial in a single column, compose an attention-grabbing headline, express a point of view and remember to include a call for some kind of action. You need to include some facts to back up your opinion, so you will have to do some research.

Choose one of the following topics:

- Improving our schools
- The influence of television
- Our greatest problem in the next ten years
- The problem of obesity in Australian teenagers

Your editorial should be approximately 250 words long.

Writing
Unit 13
A motivational speech

The purpose of a **motivational speech** is to inspire your audience or convince them to act in a particular way. The following example is the text of a speech from a health professional to parents:

Tonight, ladies and gentlemen, it's time to accept that we as a society and many of us as parents are letting down our kids. Too many of them are unfit and, in many cases, obese. As a result, they are heading towards a very unhealthy adulthood.

Our working lives are frantically busy and we have become complacent about many of our other responsibilities, including our family's health. It is often easier to be couch potatoes and to let our children be couch potatoes than to participate in fun exercise activities together. It is often easier to stuff our faces with fast food than to prepare healthy, tasty and nourishing meals for our family.

But the good news is we can easily turn this situation around. We all love our kids. We want them to be healthy and fit. We just need to make an effort to eat well and make exercise part of our family's life. We are our children's most important role models.

Okay, it's a short, simple message. For the health of our children let's make the effort to ensure that our family becomes more active and eats healthier food.

1 a In what way does the speaker want the audience to behave differently? _____

_____

b How does the speaker try to grab the audience's attention in the introduction? _____

_____

c List three emotive words or phrases that the speaker uses to make the audience feel guilty about their behaviour.

_____

_____

d How does the speaker make a point strongly in paragraph 2? _____

_____

e Which linking words does the speaker use to start the last two paragraphs? _____

_____

2 **List four arguments the speaker uses to inspire the audience to change.**

a _____

_____

b _____

_____

c ....

....

d ....

....

3 a Write an inspiring introduction for a motivational speech to encourage students in your year level to work harder at school, or to encourage teenagers to get a part-time job.

....

....

....

b List three arguments to motivate teenagers who smoke to give it up. (Only one of your arguments should be related to health.)

i ....

....

ii ....

....

iii ....

....

c You have been invited to address a sports team as a guest coach before their next match. The team has had a string of disappointing losses. Write down what you will say in your conclusion.

....

....

....

....

....

....

....

4 Choose one of the topics in Exercise 3 and write the text of the motivational speech that you would deliver. It should be approximately 250 words in length.

- Try to make your introduction inspiring.
- Use at least three different arguments to inspire your audience.
- Use at least two persuasive techniques, such as emotive words or phrases, repetition or rhetorical questions, or other methods.
- Finish your motivational speech with a strong conclusion.

Writing
Unit 14
Writing persuasively 1: the persuasive essay

Sometimes you will be asked to express your opinion on an issue and to support it with some facts and research. This is called persuasive or argumentative writing. At the end of such writing, your reader should know exactly where you stand on the issue and why you hold this view. An effective persuasive essay will:

- contain an introduction in which the writer's contention or point of view emerges clearly and strongly, which clearly defines key terms and which signals the direction the argument will take.
- contain a body that consists of at least three supporting arguments. Each of these should have its own paragraph in which the argument is explained and supported by evidence such as statistics or the opinions of people who are experts or who are directly involved. Each paragraph should be clearly linked to the next.
- contain a rebuttal paragraph in which opposing arguments are examined and shown to be wrong.
- contain a conclusion in which the arguments presented are summed-up, the contention is strongly restated and the last sentence leaves a powerful impression.

Effective persuasive essays use a range of techniques including:

Tone
Sarcastic, humorous, angry, disappointed etc.

Emotive language
This is language which positions the reader to see something in a particular way; you might refer to a new building as an 'architectural marvel' or as an 'eyesore'.

Rhetorical questions
These are questions which do not require an answer but which are used for effect; for example, 'Is it right to turn a blind eye to this kind of behaviour?'

Analogy
This is a comparison used to make the reader see a situation in a particular way; for example, 'Keeping a pit bull terrier is just like having an unexploded bomb in your backyard.'

Various appeals
Writers often use different kinds of appeals in order to argue their point of view more persuasively. These may include appeals to the reader's sense of fairness or justice: for example, 'It seems most unfair that we allow one group these rights but deny them to another section of society'. Writers may also appeal to our commonsense ('Is this a sensible plan?') our national pride ('This kind of behaviour is not what Australia is about') or our desire not to be exploited financially ('There can only be outrage that the government plans to use taxes in this way'). Many other appeals can also be made.

1 Collect an editorial or news comment piece from one of the daily papers and answer the following questions.

a What is the writer's contention or point of view? _transplant pig heart ~~needed~~ in body_

b Which key terms does the writer define? _____

c List three arguments that the writer uses to support his or her contention. _____

_____

_____

d What kind of evidence does the writer use to support his or her first argument?

_____

e Is there a rebuttal paragraph? How does the writer counter opposing arguments in this paragraph?

_____

f Identify some of the persuasive techniques used by the writer and provide an example of each one.

_____

_____

_____

2 Choose one of the following topics and then complete the following activities. You will need to do a little research and speak to people about the topic you choose.

- Should zoos be banned?
- Are single-sex schools better than co-educational schools?
- Should there be a curfew on P-plate drivers?

a Draft an introduction for your persuasive essay. What will your contention be? Which key terms will you define and how will you define them?

_____

_____

_____

_____

b List three arguments that you will use to support your contention and supply evidence in support of at least two of these arguments. Express each argument as a topic sentence.

_____

_____

_____

c Draft a rebuttal paragraph in which you examine opposing arguments and show them to be wrong.

_____

_____

_____

_____

d Draft your conclusion in which you sum-up your arguments, strongly restate your point of view and finish with a sentence that leaves the reader thinking.

_____

_____

_____

e Now write your essay off the page. Remember to make use of the range of persuasive techniques identified earlier.

Writing
Unit 15
Writing persuasively 2: using a choice of forms

You may be offered a choice of forms in which to present your point of view, and you need to understand the structure of these forms so that your response reflects the form that you have chosen. Here are some of the forms of response that are commonly offered, accompanied by a brief outline of how you can incorporate their characteristics into your own writing.

A letter to an authority involved in the issue

This should be set out as a business letter (see Unit 6). Address the person involved by the appropriate title, avoid all slang and, even though you may be angry, be polite in your approach.

A letter to the editor

These letters are generally less than 300 words in length, but responses you are asked to write at school will need to be longer. You will need to argue your case forcefully and think carefully about the tone you will use. You may write more colourfully and emotionally in this format and may comment on the views of other correspondents.

An editorial

You should be fairly conservative in your language and approach. You should adopt a knowledgeable and reasonable tone to give your editorial a greater sense of authenticity, and you should give it an appropriate headline. Because editorials are written by the senior editors of a newspaper, you could occasionally make use of phrases such as, 'At this newspaper we have always maintained ...'. You should give your editorial a heading that makes the reader think. See Unit 12 for further information.

The text of a speech

You will need to ensure that you have a clear sense of your audience. You should begin with an appropriate salutation such as, 'Thank you for being here tonight. It is a clear sign that you are parents who care'. You should make use of emotive language and rhetorical questions. You should also include expert opinions and information about how a range of people will be affected by the issue. You will probably want to create a sense of solidarity and in order to do this you should use inclusive language ('we', 'all of us' etc).

A submission

These are set out in the form of a business letter, but you will also need to make recommendations about what should happen. You will need to present these in a series of dot points.

No matter in which form you choose to express your opinion, you will need to make sure that your response follows the same structure that is required for a persuasive essay. This means that you will need an introductory paragraph, a body that contains at least two different paragraphs (each containing a topic sentence), explanation and evidence, and a conclusion.

1   Choose one of the following topics or a topic from Unit 14 for which you have not already written a response and complete the following activities. You may need to do a little research and speak to other people about the topic you choose.

- Should homework for students in Years 7 to 9 be banned?
- Should pet shops be banned?
- Should certain breeds of dog be banned?
- Should sport be compulsory in schools?

a   Write letter to the appropriate government minister arguing your point of view or write a submission to an appropriate organisation.

_____

_____

_____

_____

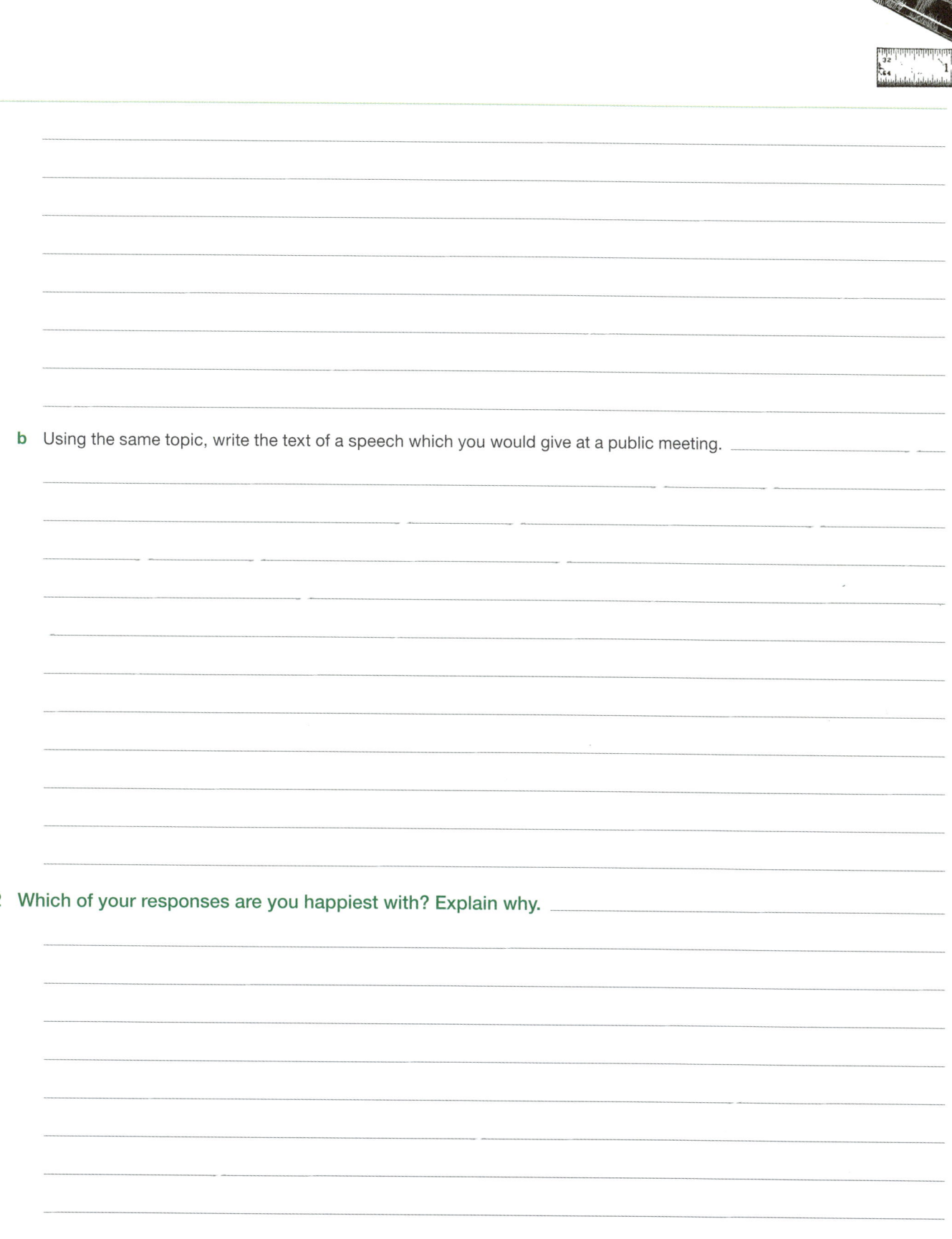

b Using the same topic, write the text of a speech which you would give at a public meeting.

2 Which of your responses are you happiest with? Explain why.

Writing

Writing
Unit 16
Essay writing: writing a text response

1 Read the question very carefully. What is it asking you to do? Underline or circle the key words.

Ask yourself: What do I know about this text which is relevant to the essay topic's key words? What is my opinion in relation to this essay topic?

At this stage, many people like to brainstorm by placing key words in the middle of a page and jotting down around them any relevant ideas.

2 **a** Brainstorm your topic off the page.

b List the points you will make in your essay in the order in which you will present them.

_____

_____

_____

3 Draft your introduction. It can be polished later but it should use the key words of the question and indicate the position you will take, briefly explaining why you agree or disagree. It is inappropriate to use the first person, for example, 'I believe that in _Lord of the Flies_ William Golding offers us some hope for the future...'. Instead you should write, 'In _Lord of the Flies_, Golding offers us some hope for the future ...'.

_____

_____

_____

_____

4   Plan the body of your essay, using TEEL (Topic sentence, Explanation, Evidence, Linking sentence). Write a topic sentence for each paragraph. Additional comments should explain this point. Remember to use examples and/or quotes from the text as evidence to support each point.

Ensure that your paragraphs are linked and that you regularly tie your comments back to the key words of the question. Aim to have four paragraphs in the body of your essay on this occasion.

1   _____

2   _____

3   _____

4   _____

5   Write a draft of your conclusion. It should sum up the position you have taken in relation to the topic and end on a powerful note.

_____

_____

_____

_____

_____

_____

_____

_____

_____

_____

_____

_____

_____

_____

_____

_____

_____

_____

6   Use this draft to write your text response essay.

Writing
Unit 17
Proofreading your writing: audience, purpose, titles, content

It is important that you check your writing specifically to ensure that you have fulfilled your stated purpose and written appropriately for your audience. You also need to check that the content has been relevant. The title of your piece needs to be interesting and relevant as well.

Audience and purpose

When you choose a topic you need to decide what your purpose and audience will be. In other words, why are you writing this piece and for whom? This will help you to be much more focused in your writing and to make some important decisions about the form in which you choose to write.

You should attach a statement of intention, which outlines your purpose, audience and any other decisions about the way you have chosen to write.

Some purposes for writing are:

- to instruct
- to inform
- to entertain
- to describe
- to persuade
- to complain.

Many pieces of writing have more than one purpose.

Titles

You need to give your writing an interesting and exciting title. Avoid boring titles such as 'My Holiday' or 'Film Review'. Your title could sum up an important idea, or you could use a line from what you have written. It should be interesting enough to make the reader want to read your piece. You should try to develop what is called a working title before you start to help you focus. If you think of something better when you finish, you can change your title. The title below, 'Pandering to the tourists', is much more intriguing than 'My Holiday' would have been. Note the pun, or play on words, on the words 'panda' and 'pander' (to indulge or play up to something).

Read the following statement of intention:

Pandering to the tourists

This is a personal piece, based on a holiday to China. My audience is my twelve-year-old granddaughter. I have chosen to tell my story in the form of an email as that is the way she would receive holiday news from overseas. My purpose is to entertain her, as well as making her aware of the plight of the pandas in China.

1 a What is the purpose of this piece? _____

_____

  b Who is the audience? _____

_____

  c What form of writing has been chosen? Why? _____

_____

2 a Devise an exciting title for each of the following.

- A review of *Star Wars Episode 3: Revenge of the Sith*.

  _____

- An editorial which argues that students have been given too much homework.

  _____

b Think of an alternative title for a TV show you have seen recently. Explain why you think this would be a good title.

_____

_____

3 Take a piece of writing that you have completed recently, reread it (preferably aloud), and ask yourself the following questions:

a Have I written a relevant and detailed statement of intention? How could it be improved?

_____

_____

b Have I chosen a relevant audience for the topic?

_____

_____

c Have I made my purpose clear? (You may have more than one purpose. For example, the piece on pandas could aim to entertain the reader as well as to inform him or her about the plight of the pandas.)

_____

_____

d Is the title of my piece interesting and relevant?

_____

_____

e Is the content of my piece appropriate for the audience and purpose?

_____

_____

f Have I chosen the best form of writing for my piece? (Some examples of forms are: newspaper article, formal letter, personal letter, email, dialogue, narrative, poem, song lyrics, submission to a group, the text for a speech.)

_____

_____

Writing

Notes

Notes

Notes